'I'm a firm believer that organisations cannot outperform their collective mindset. Jeff's book is a wonderful resource to ensure the mindset your organisation holds is aligned with optimal performance.'

Michael Henderson
Corporate Anthropologist, Cultures at Work

'This incredibly astute book will show you how to build the path to meaningful progress, projecting you and your team into a better future.'

Dr. Jason Fox
Bestselling author of *How to Lead a Quest*

'I have no doubt that projects are the missing link between strategy and execution. Projectify is a total mindset for getting things done, not simply an idea.'

Matt Church
Founder at Thought Leaders Global

'Jeff Schwisow has nailed it! This is a highly practical book on projects. But rather than joining the masses of books that talk about how to run a project, he focuses on how to use projects in your organise to drive strategy forward. I firmly believe that projects are how we get our most meaningful work done, and Projectify *provides a simple framework to create relevant and impactful projects that get results.'*

Dermot Crowley
Author of *Smart Work*

'When Jeff explains that productivity is regarded more highly than creativity, I can't help but remember reading "Imagination is more important than knowledge" by Einstein.

Jeff is himself a renaissance man of our times.

Projectify *transcends its title. Elevating the reader from mere mechanistic understanding of project management to a more purposeful and meaningful business leadership. I speak here not from theoretical concepts rather from real hands-on experience. Jeff has helped me navigate the shifting sands of business in several companies and mega projects across Australia.*

Over the years Jeff has facilitated the conversion of my teams. From attempting to deliver on a staid KPI compliant "Strategic Business Plan" to a dynamic portfolio of real improvement projects. Involving a collegiate team of knowledge workers as opposed to commanding a group of drones. Creating momentum for a constant and incremental improvement mindset.

Jeff always encouraged me to spend more time on the field and less on the scoreboard. A simple but very powerful concept.

This book is full of powerful practical tools distilled from many years of challenges overcome.

Read it and buy your team a copy too!'

Duncan Whitfield
Western Field Operations Manager,
Powercor Network Services

'Jeff is an expert in projects and making them happen well – that is clear from the insight, guidance and logic he outlines in this book. Organisations are constantly struggling with the challenge of delivering more, with less resources (time, people and money). By adopting what Jeff terms an 'evolutionary business mindset' you can make the advancements you need to keep up or stride ahead of the competition.

His book is highly practical and easy to read, making it an ideal reference source for leaders who are looking to break the curse of the "business of busyness".'

Michelle Gibbings
Founder and Managing Director of Change Meridian;
Author of *Step Up: How to Build Your Influence at Work*

'In a world of constant change, where we are all tasked with coming up with new ideas and then bringing them to life, the need to work together collaboratively on projects that truly matter is key. Jeff's book and thinking around how we build exceptional workplaces is quite simply awesome, and a must read for anyone building businesses for the future.'

Janine Garner
Founder and CEO of LBD Group;
Author of *It's Who You Know* and *From Me to We*

JEFF SCHWISOW

PROJECTIFY

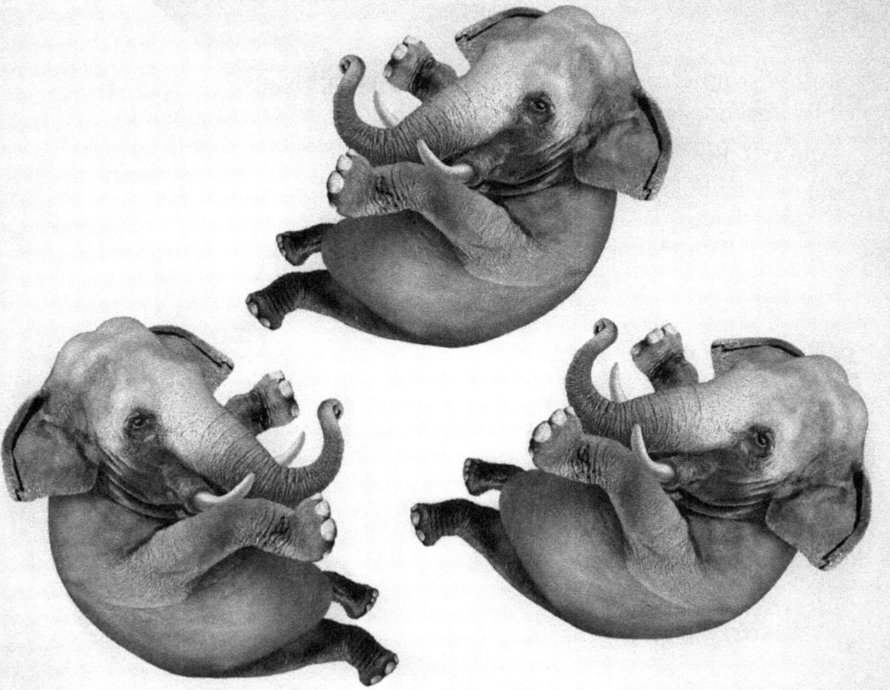

How to use projects to engage your people in strategy that evolves your business

Published in 2017

A CIP catalogue of this book is available from the National Library of Australia.

ISBN: 978-0-9953777-7-6

Editing and publishing by Kelly Irving
kellyirving.com

Cover design and internal layout by Ellie Schroeder
ellieschroeder.com

jeffschwisow.com

JEFFSCHWISOW

CONTENTS

About the author

Jeff Schwisow is passionate about people and projects.

It's when the two come together that a truly exceptional workplace is formed – one that engages the very best of its people, one that consistently delights its clients and one that constantly evolves to generate exceptional business results by being exceptional.

Over the last 30 years, Jeff has lived and breathed projects – leading them, studying them, fixing them and making them sing. He has helped businesses across a number of industries to use projects better and to do better projects, including Shell, Chevron, PetroChina, CPB Contractors and many more.

His current writing, speaking, mentoring and strategic development work helps teams tap into their true potential to see projects not as a risk to be managed, but as an investment in the future that they aspire to create.

jeffschwisow.com

In gratitude

As this book neared completion and I sat down to write the 'Acknowledgements' section, what poured out of me was not merely acknowledgement but deep gratitude – a recognition and heart-felt gratefulness for all those people who have allowed me to stand at the threshold of a feat I would have never dreamed possible.

These people believed so strongly in creating a better world in which to work and live that I too came to believe that my ideas were worth adding to their knowledge and wisdom.

Perhaps many authors before me have felt this moment – a visceral appreciation for the collective consciousness that made their book possible. So firstly, to all of you, I would like to say thanks. Without those who have dared for centuries to put their ideas out into the world for all to see – whether that world is populated by hundreds or millions – it would be impossible for those of us following in your footsteps. I hope I've done my part in honouring that tradition.

So many acknowledgements finish with the readers, but for me it doesn't end with them; it starts with them. For without an audience – someone whom the author is trying to touch in some way – a book has no soul. So huge thanks to everyone that reads this book, whether in whole or in part. I'm especially grateful to those of you who ponder the ideas it contains and use them to stimulate the conversation about the future of work – the relationships that businesses have with their people and the investment that people are willing to make in their workplace. If you think enough of these ideas to pass this book along to someone else who might take inspiration from them, then you hold a very special place in my heart.

This book would not have been possible without the small but mighty team of professionals who turned my ramblings and undisciplined intentions into a project (imagine!) to commit my thinking to the page. A huge thank you to my editor and book project leader, Kelly Irving. Your ability to cut through my verbal diarrhoea to bring clarity, voice and story in service of the reader was extraordinary. Without your expertise, guidance, and passion this wouldn't be half the book it is today. Without your periodic kicks in the arse, it would still be languishing in the "one day" pile in which so many books sit. Thanks to Patrick and Ellie for the exceptional quality and style they brought to the finished product. Also, a huge shout-out to Dan Cruceanu, the graphic designer who came up with the original cover concept.

I would also like to thank everyone who has taught or encouraged me to continuously expand my thinking – to challenge the status quo, to ask important and unanswered questions, to become comfortable with discomfort. Thank you to the important teachers in my life who have taught me that education has little to do with test scores, grades or degrees – that it's about maintaining a mind open to learning and creating. From my 7th grade science teacher, Joe Satakasy, who showed his classes that not only science but life too is about experimentation and testing hypotheses, to my college physics professor, Dr. Donald Ziebell, who made us sit exams without calculators because he wanted us to 'see' the solution not just manipulate the numbers. Thanks to Drs. Oliver, Gater and Shih in the University of Florida's Mechanical Engineering Department, who taught me that engineering was about solving problems not just answering questions – which means being comfortable with assumption and uncertainty, but uncomfortable with things that aren't useful.

I'm grateful to Paul Gandy, who as a fellow intern in a consulting engineering office in 1981 accepted my 'invitation' to help paint the interior of my 3-bedroom rental house without blinking an eye before he even knew me. Over the next 12 or so years, Paul helped me find an appreciation for playing music, making and drinking margaritas and challenging what I thought myself capable of – both personally and professionally. Paul taught me to aspire to something larger than myself. Even though we haven't worked together for over 20 years, you're still the best friend I've ever had.

I'd like to acknowledge and thank some of the great authors and speakers who, over the years, have shaped and inspired my thinking and opened up new vistas from which to perceive the world: the writings of Carlos Castaneda; everything ever written or said by Seth Godin; *Start with Why* and *Leaders Eat Last* by Simon Sinek; *The Black Swan* and *Antifragile* by Nassim Nicholas Taleb; *The Progress Principle* by Teresa Amabile and Steven Kramer; *Drive* by Dan Pink; *The 7 Habits of Highly Effective People* by Stephen Covey; *Flow* by Mihaly Csikszentmihalyi; *Chiefing Your Tribe and Above the Line* by Michael Henderson; *Outliers* and *The Tipping Point* by Malcolm Gladwell; and for all those who seek to create and inspire change in the world: *Grit* by Angela Duckworth; *Deep Work* by Cal Newport; *Mindset* by Carol Dweck; and *The War of Art* and *Nobody Wants to Read Your Sh*t* by Steven Pressfield.

Were it not for the amazing community at Thought Leaders Business School, I would still be trapped by the belief that my value to the world is defined by what I have done, not by what I think and believe. Thank you for your unbending commitment to standing up for each other and your belief that we can collectively change the consciousness of the planet – it has made me constantly seek to be the very best version of myself. In particular, I am grateful to Matt Church, who named this book before a single word was on the page, and who saw greater possibilities in me than I saw in myself. He taught me to dare to play a bigger game. Peter Cook, the dean of TLBS, provided me with an implementation framework (and tough love accountability) that helped me to start getting shit done in my practice, rather than waiting for it to happen. Through his book *The New Rules of Management*, Peter also had a significant impact on the thinking that shaped my own projectification framework. I'm also grateful for the many people who have advised, encouraged, inspired, promoted and drank with me on my TLBS journey: Dr Andrew Pratley, whose collaboration taught me the power of asking good questions and extracting important answers; Paul Broadfoot, Bryan Whitefield, Jonathon Reeve, Kieran Flanagan, Dermot Crowley, Janine Garner, Mykel Dixon, Michelle Gibbings, Col and Cam Fink and my mentor, Rohan Dredge.

A special acknowledgement must go to Dr. Jason Fox for his profound impact on my thinking and this book. Jason's books *Game Changer* and *How to Lead a Quest* provided both affirmation for my own ideas and new perspectives from which to view the future of work and the workplace. Furthermore, his writing and speaking are such an authentic and unapologetic expression of who he is that it forces me to constantly seek and express myself in my own work – albeit from two quite different but complimentary universes.

Now I must express my gratitude for those people whom I most hold dear – my family and friends.

To my amazing wife, Heather, who endured all the late nights, early mornings, vacant dinner conversations and drifting attention on holidays. You have been a supporter, reviewer, coach and occasional disciplinarian when I needed to get my head screwed on straight. You helped me find my way to the light when it was darkest. You helped me find belief when I was drowning in doubt. I could not have written this book without you, nor would I want to.

Thanks to my incredibly supportive friends Mark, Michela, Mike, Nicole and Natalie, who have put up with me rabbiting on about all things thought leadership and have diligently read my blog since its inception. My life and this book are the better for the friendship and discourse you so generously share with me.

Last, but certainly not least, I owe an unrepayable debt of gratitude to my parents Faye and Howard. Without their love, sacrifice, encouragement and support, I would not be the person I am today and it is unlikely I would have followed the path that I find myself on. To a bright but unruly, undisciplined kid, they gave grounding, opportunity and a model of behaviour that was a rare blessing. As a youth, I strayed far and wide but they maintained an unwavering beacon of light and love that helped me to find my way. My father, in particular, showed me what it means to be a man, a father and a husband – no mere titles, but responsibilities to be taken seriously every single day. They have shown me that no matter your starting point, no matter your resources, that hard work, dedication and service to those around you will create a better future for those who matter most: your family.

Introduction

'My team is struggling to develop a strategy that differs from what we've always done; one that moves with the times and the market.'

'We're so engaged in the day-to-day, the immediate and urgent work, that we have no time or energy to devote to what might be ahead; in some cases, what we KNOW is ahead.'

'Even when we do manage to set out a strategic direction, we see a lot of activity but little progress that translates into meaningful business outcomes.'

'If I do manage to get my people onboard with a new strategy, I spend all my energy struggling against resistance to the change.'

These are things I hear executives and CEOs of large organisations say on a regular basis.

Strategy was (and still is for some) about creating a three- or five-year plan focused on plotting a specific course into the future based on the conditions that are known today. When things don't go according to that plan, we panic and revert to what we've always done – wrapping ourselves in the deceptive comfort of 'core business'.

For others, strategy is all about aspiration – setting lofty business targets and creating catchy slogans. Yet the 'business of busyness' – meeting-filled calendars, a steady stream of crises, and reporting cycles that each begin before the last one ends – often quickly consumes the time and attention it would take to translate this aspiration into action and activity.

The business environment is changing. Sure, everything moves faster than ever before. But that has been true for decades – for a long time, the 'current' environment has been more dynamic than ever before. What is different in today's business world is the pervasiveness of that dynamism. Now it is not just so-called disrupted industries or single elements of your business that are being impacted by the pace of change. It is happening everywhere, in every industry and at every level of your business.

The rules are changing because waiting to react to your environment puts you perilously behind in a race that punishes those who can't maintain the pace. The question now is not 'How do I keep up?' but 'How do I forward-focus and project into the future so that I am leading from the front, driving change instead of responding to it?'.

In today's dynamic world, strategy needs to be a continuous process of re-shaping your business for a future that you want to become. Effective strategic activity relies on understanding the disruptive forces and emerging opportunities that lie outside our control. It is about counteracting those forces and actively seizing those opportunities.

It is no longer good enough to do what you've always done and make it bigger, or do it more productively. Now you have to *evolve* what you do – what you make – as the market and the environment changes.

It used to be that businesses were either 'growing or dying' but in today's world they are either 'evolving or declining'.

As a CEO, leader or executive of a mid-to-large organisation with a traditional top-down approach that has been successful to date, you don't need convincing of this.

You recognise the imperative to change your thinking and strategic approach to be future-focused – to have a strategy for evolving and adapting as your business changes and as the business environment continues to change.

The real question is: How?

How do you create space in your leadership team's busy schedule for deep strategic thought?

How do you effectively engage your workforce to make your strategic intent an operational reality?

The approach that served us well in the first half of the 20th century was a **growth business mindset**, in which you see the majority of your people as foot soldiers whom you direct to carry out the core business. You:

» Tell them what you want them to do.

» Incentivise them to do it well.

» Drive productivity and scale.

But today requires a new approach, an **evolutionary business mindset**, where you bring the business and your people together to leverage the bandwidth and capabilities of the entire organisation so you can constantly adapt. You:

» Engage and motivate people by giving them something to be engaged in and meaningful progress to be motivated by.

» Attract and retain customers by genuinely caring about their constantly shifting and ever-more demanding wants and needs.

» Create a future that the business can evolve into.

This book will show you how to make strategic activity and constant adaptation a part of your enterprise's operational fabric. It will show you how to adopt this evolutionary business mindset.

You'll learn to use projects and a project mindset to create a bridge between your business and the people in your business, to bring them together so that they are not separate entities but working as one, together in harmony.

You'll learn to leverage their leadership bandwidth – their time, attention and energy – to create a culture where your people are the driving force behind excellence: excellence in the workplace, as well as in business performance, to produce a culture of greatness.

> You'll learn how projectifying strategic activity will turn into something that's real and intentional – moving from strategic intent to strategic action.

I love creating truly exceptional workplaces where people come together – feeding off diverse ideas and experiences – to do truly amazing things. I've helped many businesses and business leaders like you to create working environments where the business and its people both serve and are served by each other, in equal measure.

At its core, this is a book about creating those sorts of workplaces. Places where businesses value their people and the people in those businesses value the opportunities created by a thriving business. The sort of workplaces that create great business because they constantly deliver great value to the customers they serve.

These ideas presented in this book have helped many organisations – both large and small – do that, and they can help you too.

So let's look at how you can use projects to engage your people in strategic activity that evolves your business, today.

PART I
STRATEGY

The early 20th century saw the development of a more 'scientific' approach to managing the large corporations that were beginning to form in the post-Industrial Revolution world.

This new corporate world needed a way of bringing scale and efficiency to the largely repetitive work that had previously been the domain of craft-based shops and small mom-and-pop businesses. In this new management revolution, managing the business became a profession that was separated from the work of the business – thinking was separated from doing.

Although there have been refinements and technological advances, many of the core tenets of these management approaches are largely unchanged since the turn of the 20th century. There is certainly sense in why they have endured. Firstly, they work – or at least have proven to be pretty effective over quite a long period of time. Secondly, they are what we know – for our entire lives, we have only ever been taught one way to manage a business. Finally, there is comfort in tradition – the familiar, well-worn path seems certain to lead us where we want to go.

This relatively slow rate of development of management thinking is in direct contrast to the ever-faster pace of change in the business environment it is meant to respond to. So in the first part of this book, we'll talk about how the rate of business change is reaching a tipping point where the traditional reactionary response leaves you hopelessly behind with no time to catch up.

We'll also discuss how a range of concepts applied to this scientific management approach were drawn from the military tradition, which had been undertaking large complex endeavours for centuries. Chief among these military adaptations were the ideas of organisational hierarchies and of developing strategy separate from tactics. However, we have distorted these concepts as we refined them over the years. Strategy, in particular, has become a very static activity detached from tactical action. It has taken on a very analytical focus that is more about maintaining the past than adapting in the present in order to move toward a sustainable future.

Then we'll set the scene for a different way of thinking about your business future. We'll talk about why projectifying strategic execution is the remedy for today's world of dynamic business change. Through the effective use of projects, you can reclaim strategy as a process and not just an event.

> You can reconnect strategic thinking to tactical action. You can evolve your business as the environment unfolds before you.

1

The case for change

A 'Kodak moment' has long meant (and still does for many) a moment in time that cries out to be captured and savoured. It has nothing to do with the type of camera, film or paper you're using.

Yet Kodak went from being a leading company, once dominant in its field of photography, to one forced to file for bankruptcy in 2012. Digital photography and videography signalled the end of film-based images, then the advent of digital sharing and streaming put a hole in Kodak's printing consumables business. For their part, the company didn't adequately anticipate or respond to that disruptive threat. Now all that remains is their catch-cry.

On the surface, this is probably an accurate summarisation of Kodak's history, but the truth about their fall is much more complex and subtle. They weren't blind-sided by a technology they never saw coming; in fact, Kodak built the first digital camera in 1975.

They also didn't miss the impact that the internet would have on the way that photos are shared and experienced. In 2001, they purchased a photo-sharing site, Ofoto. However, instead of using their new EasyShare Gallery as a means of connecting people through photos and videos, the focus of the site was on trying to get users to print digital images.

Kodak had been selling retail consumer products – cameras, slide protectors, printers and developing equipment – for several decades. Their consumer products evolved a number of times as technology and customer needs evolved – sometimes successfully and sometimes not, much like any retail product company.

What led to the decline of Kodak was their inability to translate strategic thinking and market awareness into effective business action and activity.

Kodak failed to create a business vision and purpose that were not tied to producing physical images. They were unable to create a culture where their people saw *beyond* showing up for work every day just to do more of what they had always done – a culture where they sought to ideate, create and experiment in a realm outside of what they already knew.

As an organisation, they struggled to embrace small, agile shifts of direction to explore where new strategic opportunities might exist. Kodak constantly bet big on new products and new markets, but largely as a follower rather than a leader. The resulting new divisions were then retracted to 'core business' when these multi-million dollar transformational changes failed to pay off.

In *The Real Lessons from Kodak's Decline*, Willy Shih, a senior vice president at Eastman Kodak Co. and president of the company's consumer digital business from 1997 to 2003 says:

> Senior leaders at Kodak were acutely aware of the approaching storm. I know because I arrived at Kodak from Silicon Valley in mid-1997, just as digital photography was taking off. Management was constantly tracking the rate at which digital media was replacing film. But several factors made it exceedingly difficult for Kodak to shift gears and emerge with a consumer franchise that would be sustainable over the long term. Not only was a major technological change upending our competitive landscape; challenges were also affecting the ecosystem we operated in and our organizational model. Ultimately, refocusing the business with so many forces in motion proved to be impossible.

Don't let this be you and your business.

How will you respond?

Business change has long been synonymous with strategic shifts initiated by the organisation. But in today's cause-and-effect world, business change is no longer a choice. Your business responds to this evolving dynamic whether you choose to or not.

Now the question is not 'if' but 'how' that response will occur. Will it happen as an uncontrolled reaction to an external force, or as a calculated move to minimise the impact of that force? Are you reactive or proactive? Are your initiatives aimed at innovating and leading your market, or trying to keep up?

Most of today's organisations focus on 'maintaining' their core business. They might look for growth opportunities or productivity improvements, but they are firmly invested in staying the course that has gotten them to where they are.

They see their future as a bright, shiny reflection of their present and/or their past. Most enterprises only initiate change when problems with their profitability, top-line growth or market share tell them they have to – but by then it's already too late. The market has moved on, leaving them behind.

Your challenge, as a leader, is to take control of the direction of that change and create an opportunity to adapt to adverse conditions before they negatively impact you and your bottom line.

The danger in business today

The potential threats that your business faces right now might not be as dramatic as the ones faced by Kodak. The landscape in which your business operates might not be shifting so significantly that it means you must completely re-shape your business focus.

On the other hand, the shifts now occurring might be subtler and less apparent than in the photography and film-making industries of the late 20th century. This means that the potential impacts might be just as significant now as they were back then – you just don't see them.

As just about every business book currently written will tell you, the pace of change in today's business environment is greater than it has ever been. However, this ever-increasing rate of change – its exponential nature – is not unique to the early 21st century. It has been occurring for several decades now. In the 1980s, uses for the worldwide web were limited and reserved for the select few. By the 1990s, email was everywhere and portals for accessing this growing network of information were popping up every day. In the early 1990s, a mobile telephone was the size of a toaster and cost as much as a car – but by the mid-2000s, it had more computing power than an Apollo spacecraft and came practically free with your mobile service.

What is unique today is the number of moving parts in the business landscape that are impacted by change. It is no longer a single element of your business that is impacted – a single change can ripple across all of your business. The market shifts faster than ever as competitors and products enter and leave it. Customer needs and wants continually shift and evolve – they expect more as their choices grow. Technology affects more and more areas within your business. It's no longer internal implementation challenges but external impacts that we need to respond to. Meanwhile, globalisation creates economic shockwaves that move around the world at alarming speed.

The danger with today's pace of change is that a great many industries are reaching a tipping point. Once you have fallen behind, it is no longer possible to catch up. If you miss the wave, you can't paddle fast enough to hop back on. When Kodak saw digital photography starting to take off and supplant film, they had time to move into a leadership position in the digital market. However, since their fortunes were still tied to film-based products as smartphone technology and social media converged, their opportunity to adapt had already passed them by.

Today's business environment can change like a powerful and persistent rising tide – one that could turn into a tsunami of disruption at any given time.

Competition now comes from non-traditional sources that force us to completely rethink how to deliver what our customers demand. Uber, the world's largest transportation company, doesn't own any vehicles and Airbnb, the world's largest accommodation provider, doesn't own any property. The fact that these businesses didn't exist 10 years ago suggests we must constantly redefine what our customers want and what our market is.

These market shifts are not confined to what you might think of as 'volatile industries' such as technology or consumer products. They have been (and are!) occurring in industries that have been firmly entrenched for decades. The shopping centre is moving from being a retail outlet to a showroom for what we buy online – a place where we gather to socialise rather than purchase. Banking is starting to see new competitors whose focus is helping customers manage their finances toward their life goals rather than just a place to store, borrow or transfer money.

Even construction, one of the largest and most staid industries in the world, is about to come under innovative pressures from artificial intelligence, the manufacturing sector and 3D printing technologies – not just ever-larger and more sophisticated construction equipment.

Just like Kodak missed the move to digital imaging, you too may struggle to swim with whatever's coming if you don't have the right foresight and strategic direction.

Your tipping point

In The Tipping Point, *Malcolm Gladwell discusses the idea that a great many phenomena – disease, ideas, commercial products – can go from steady but modest growth to exponential growth under the influence of a particular catalyst. He argues that these phenomena reach a certain point where they 'tip' – when the innovation or idea moves from the part of a population known as the Early Adopters into the Early Majority.*

The Early Adopters are visionaries who are willing take risks in order to drive revolutionary change: in business, these tend to be smaller companies. By contrast, the Early Majority are careful pragmatists looking to minimise risk in search of incremental, progressive change: in business, these characteristically tend to be larger organisations. These fundamental differences mean that Early Adopters and the Early Majority don't talk to each other – visionaries want to share their excitement with other visionaries and pragmatists want to evaluate the experiences of other pragmatists.

For a long time, this chasm created a natural barrier to disruptive influences for medium to large organisations. They could rest secure in the knowledge that their competition and the market more generally sat firmly in the pragmatic, Early (to Late) Majority camp. There was a very limited communication link with the Early Adopters and, as a result, a relatively slow diffusion of new influences making it across the chasm. Importantly, the initial diffusion into the Early Majority population tended to be relatively slow and undertaken in a cautious manner as enough evidence was gathered to get this group talking about it with their fellow pragmatists.

However, this is no longer the case.

The communication chasm between the Early Adopters and the Early Majority - between the visionaries and the pragmatists – is being bridged.

Greater access to capital means that Early Adopters are no longer the small gun-slinging start-ups of an earlier era. More frequently, Innovators are being brought into the mainstream by Early Adopters such as larger organisations or more influential customer groups, because they are willing to invest in the visionary thinking that allows them to disrupt existing markets.

Development of agile project approaches means that innovations and new ideas can be developed and scaled much more quickly and at lower risk than ever before, enabling the pragmatic Early Majority to have their cake and eat it too. They can be quicker to adopt without the risk profile of a visionary. As a result, the true Early Majority is much more tapped into the Innovators and the Early Adopters – closing the chasm with much more open communication.

New innovations are much more closely tied to legacy systems and work methods, so they no longer have to cross the chasm from an old operating system to a new operating system – one is the extension of the other.

Today's rapid flow of information means that your customers (and consumers more broadly) are much more educated about those innovations finding a beachhead with the Early Adopters. They are much more likely to connect with their experiences and be bullish about the relative risk and reward of moving with them. As this appeal shrinks in your customers' world, ideas and innovations diffuse much quicker and can be transformed into majority expectations seemingly overnight. Before you have an opportunity to respond, this desire is being served by someone else.

Most importantly, many of the changes and shifts diffusing through the business environment are no longer confined to a unique technology, a single remote corner of your operation or a specific segment of your customer base. The intertwining of new innovation with traditional systems and practices can mean change impacts your entire business ecosystem. As new competitors go from asking customers what they want to completely re-defining it, adding a new feature to what you make is an inadequate competitive response.

As a result, it is no longer safe for businesses to nurture the chasm of communication between themselves and the visionaries, just waiting to join a market trend or respond to competitive influence once their fellow pragmatists demonstrate that it is a safe path to follow. Today, it is far more likely that once you see that a business shift is 'safe' for the majority, it has already reached a tipping point. And once it has tipped, organisations can very quickly find themselves in the Late Majority or, worse yet, the Laggards scrambling to repair the damage and try to keep up with the shift.

Now versus next

It is easy to see disruptive forces and the ever-increasing pace of change as the enemy that your business must defeat.

The real enemy of business evolution is not change, but how 'now' cripples your ability to focus on 'next'.

The multitude of forces (both life forces and our genetic predisposition) that push us into the immediate and urgent prevent us from being able to create the time to forward think.

More than at any point in history, time and attention are your most valuable resources. The demands of the immediate and urgent are greater than they have ever been. The growing volume of information that must be processed in our hyper-connected world is placing unprecedented demands on the attention of today's business leaders. This focus then spreads through the enterprise as a reflection of what is perceived as important.

The good news is that we are genetically wired for this type of reactionary environment. For millennia, our foremost concerns were the immediate need to find food, maintain our shelters and be constantly on the lookout for danger so that we didn't get eaten.

When faced with an urgent threat or emerging crisis, we get physically aroused through the release of adrenaline and cortisol. This allows us to spring into action and face the challenge or flee quickly (but, of course, you're not that kind of leader). We get a little psychological pleasure from the dopamine hit that accompanies this arousal. We get a sense of satisfaction from a day filled with problem-solving because of the in-built release of serotonin.

The stakes aren't quite as high today as they were for our ancestors. You are unlikely to get physically eaten while solving the daily challenges in your business. However, it does imply that the immediate and urgent isn't just a condition that exists within your business environment; it's also a physiological trap we are pre-disposed to fall into.

The beauty of problems that come flowing into your office – via the phone or email or unexpected visitors – is that you don't have to go searching for them. You can turn on your reactive brain and let your instincts take over. There is also a strong sense of accomplishment that comes from a day filled with putting out fires, solving pressing problems or getting through your to-do list.

The bad news is that in a time- and attention-poor world, future-focused work gets pushed into the background or gets relegated by the administration of the day-to-day. As a result, most organisations don't acknowledge a problem or a threat until it is a BIG problem or threat – one that has confirmed its existence by manifesting itself as a negative business performance result. Even more importantly, new ideas and opportunities don't get serious attention until the market – or a competitor – has demonstrated their viability. More often than not, this demonstration is couched in terms of some type of emerging business challenge.

To take advantage of our affinity for the immediate, we need to bring the next into the now.

We must bring the future into the present to take advantage of how we allocate our time and attention, and to make strategy part of what you do every day.

First, we need to agree on what an effective strategy is in the modern business. We need to understand what it's meant to accomplish in today's dynamic business environment and how it's meant to accomplish it.

Projectify points

1. The business environment that you operate in today constantly shifts and changes. The pace of that change is faster than ever, but the greatest challenge is the pervasive impact of this change.

2. Your business will respond to this dynamic whether you choose to or not – the goal is to take control of that response rather than have it control you.

3. The multitude of forces that push you into immediate and urgent responses prevent you from being able to create the time – and, more importantly, the attention – to be future-focused.

4. The real enemy of business evolution is not change, but how 'now' cripples your ability to focus on 'next'.

5. The impacts of this changing business environment have reached a tipping point – if you fall behind now there is no longer opportunity to catch up.

6. You need to use these forces to become allies that your business enlists to help it thrive.

An illusion of certainty

Most of the future-focused work we do today falls under the auspices of strategic planning. We hope to transform an uncertain business environment into a certain future by setting firm targets and a plan to achieve those targets.

This analytical approach is heavily focused on actions the business will take to elicit a pre-conceived response from the market. It largely ignores that markets are far too dynamic for a cause-and-effect approach – where customers will choose to spend their money and where the competitive forces will come from are fickle propositions.

Strategy has not always been this way. Business strategy, as we know it today, has its roots in military strategy. In military terms, strategic planning was conceived in the knowledge that the environment you were campaigning in was highly uncertain and constantly changing. To be successful in this environment, your future thinking needed to be fluid and constantly adapting to conditions and events as they unfolded.

Military strategists recognised that this high-level thinking (using battles to win wars) was different from tactics (managing troops to win battles).

The technical details around military strategy have evolved from the first century BC to the present day, but have maintained a set of common themes:

» Differentiate strategy from tactics, but don't separate them – use one to inform the other.

» Strategic direction is meant to serve a policy objective – an overarching purpose – not a specific result or outcome. In this sense, strategy-making and governance are intertwined.

» Strategy-making is a continuous process and not meant as a means of generating an output (i.e., plans or KPIs or vision statements) – it is ever-evolving as tactical results manifest themselves and, as a result, policy objectives also evolve.

The scientific management movement in the early 20th century adopted many of the military concepts around strategy to the management of business. However, in its evolution, this strategic link diverged from these military themes in almost every aspect. Strategy has become quite separated from the tactical – the operational world.

So business strategy has become a very static, analytical discipline – moving from an 'execute and learn' methodology to a 'plan and measure' routine. Strategy-making has transformed from an ongoing process in pursuit of a purpose to a series of events focused on producing an output. In today's businesses, strategy is something you have rather than something you do.

Who are you competing against?

'Strategy exists because there is competition. Without competition, there would be no need for strategy.'

There is a profundity to this quote by Kenichi Ohmae, a Japanese strategist, that is not immediately obvious. In military strategy, the competition is either the enemy (in times of war) or an opposing nation-state (in times of peace). In the traditional business strategy approach, it is the identified competitor that you are trying to outmanoeuvre or squeeze out.

More and more in today's business environment, your competition is not the other business that does the same things you do.

Your real competition is change. It is the shifting business landscape in which you operate. Your competition is also a lack of change – the apathy or inertia that stops your customers from moving away from the status quo because change is not a compelling proposition for them.

Your most formidable competition is when your customers decide that they no longer want to buy the category in which you work – when the market disappears, as was the case of film photography for Kodak. It doesn't matter whether that market change occurs because new entrants begin to serve your customers in a different way or because economic fortunes mean that your clients don't see value in investing in your product or service.

Competition comes when there is a market shift in what customers value about your category. When they determine that 'best' in your category is equally distributed, then differentiation becomes price – your product or service becomes a commodity. A commoditised market is a competition that few businesses win in the long-term without the ability to redefine what customers value as 'best' or an effective means of owning the low-cost space.

Today's most effective strategy-making is not about defeating the competition that you know, but about preparing and adapting your business for the change that is coming.

As Sun Tzu said in The Art of War:

> *So it is said that if you know your enemies and know yourself, you will not be put at risk even in a hundred battles.*
>
> *If you only know yourself, but not your opponent, you may win or may lose.*
>
> *If you know neither yourself nor your enemy, you will always endanger yourself.*

What's your plan?

Since the 1960s, this analytical perspective on business strategy development has become standard management practice for every large corporation in the developed world. For most businesses, the standard purpose of strategy development is to come up with a 'strategic plan'.

> There is a need, at all levels of an enterprise, to have a carefully crafted plan to demonstrate that its senior leadership team has its hands firmly on the reins of the future.

Strategy-making activities are largely centred on what have been termed *strategic planning* and *strategic thinking*. The logic here makes perfect sense in that you need to conceive a strategy – the *thinking* bit – before you can plan it. The problem is that, although rich in planning and analysis, these are low on strategic action.

Most organisations schedule strategic development sessions at particular times in the business calendar. These sessions generally follow a carefully structured strategic development process that boasts a 'big couple of days with a jam-packed agenda'. Central to this process is the setting of business targets and performance goals for a one-, three- or five-year 'business planning horizon', then analysing the current business environment or, more likely, the historical operational environment, to formulate the strategic activities required to meet these targets and goals.

This formulation is then shaped into a strategic plan that outlines the resources, expenditures and timeframes for bringing the strategy to life. Typically, the strategic plan will outline broad strategic initiatives such as capital or systems investments, market expansion plans and sales expectations of these strategic changes. Many of the best strategic plans include competitor analysis, market research and some manner of risk and opportunity analysis as data to support the anticipated business results.

One of the primary reasons for the heavy analytical focus is that nothing creates the impression of good governance better than a detailed plan flush with financial targets and analysis that demonstrates a clear path to reach those targets. Sprinkle in a vision and mission statement that includes a heavy dose of corporate-speak and a lengthy SWOT analysis; suddenly, you have a document that any board would be happy with and a 'strategy' that any executive team can defend as effective corporate governance.

This carefully constructed strategic plan is often the work of the business strategy team or a handpicked contingent of select senior staff, who develop and refine it under the watchful eye of the executive leadership team. Once finalised and approved by the executive (and perhaps the board), the strategy is now firmly in place. It is then 'communicated' to middle management and/or the organisation – usually as a one-off event – who are given responsibility for executing it.

As the year rolls on, the majority of this carefully conceived strategy is obliterated by the demands of the day-to-day work to maintain the operational status quo – until the start of the next strategic planning cycle, when the process is repeated.

Is this ringing any bells for you?

Strategy struggles

If you've struggled to implement your strategic plan, you're not alone.

Research shows that the success rate for the implementation of strategic plans is dismal, with the percentage of failed implementations ranging anywhere from 63% to 90%, depending on the research. In fact, Robert Kaplan of Balanced Scorecard fame (1996, 2000, 2008) estimates that 90% of strategies fail due to poor execution.

McKinsey & Co have found that only 23% of companies use a formal process to operationalise important strategic decisions. In 52% of companies, these decisions are made by a small senior group and poorly communicated to the rest of the organisation.

As the business world becomes ever more dynamic and strategic planning cycles shorten (from five- to three-, two- or even one-year plans are now the norm), it becomes even more difficult for your business to connect a high-level strategic plan with execution; particularly, when 'the plan' doesn't include a strategy for carrying it out.

It doesn't make a difference – why?

So why does such a carefully planned, thoroughly researched document, which dutifully incorporates a vision and mission with sources of new revenue or improvements, usually end up languishing on the managing director's shelf, never to be seen again?

It isn't truly future-focused

Central to this process is the setting of business targets and performance. You'll analyse the current business environment or, more likely, the historical operational performance to formulate the strategic activities required to meet these targets and goals.

The key phrases here are current business environment and historical operational performance.

This means that most of what goes into a strategic plan is effectively a manifesto on continuing to do what you have always done.

Albeit perhaps doing more of it, doing it in more places or in a more efficient manner.

It isn't adaptive

In today's business world, truly effective governance is more about having a strategy for adapting to change and variability than being able to predict the future and executing a plan that makes that prediction come true.

Plans can't account for the iterative nature of experimentation and testing new ideas that comes with pioneering new products, services and markets.

It lacks action

This formulation is then shaped into a strategic plan that outlines the resources, expenditures and timeframes for implementing this strategy.

Yet without a clear pathway to turn strategic intent into operational action and activity, your organisation doesn't have a strategy - not one that is alive and shaping your business outcomes.

Most importantly, there is little to inspire the organisation to action or to serve as a guidepost for a thriving, new business direction.

Strategic planning outputs that lack 'a plan' to refresh the strategy or connect your organisation to its realisation cannot possibly have life – your strategy won't be imbued with action.

It doesn't engage your people

The strategic plan is usually the closely-held responsibility of high-level management. They often take on the role of monitoring the measurement and reporting against performance targets or KPIs or scorecards that are embodied in this plan, rather than leading its implementation.

This means the day-to-day decision-making of your people is disconnected from strategic considerations. Their accumulated collective knowledge is not being brought to bear on development of your strategic direction.

> Your people are largely left to their own devices in figuring out how to deliver the desired results.

Their focus becomes creating the *perception of results* rather than the important strategic work of shaping the business for a desired future state or providing signals that allow the business to understand where the brightest future might lie.

A helicopter view

A common misconception about business strategy is that it is purely a high-level activity – a helicopter perspective on your business. Because most of what goes into a strategic plan is based on analysis of the current or, more likely, the historical operational environment, we replace future-focused strategy and tactics with the management and execution of operational activities.

As a result, we confuse strategic development with high-level operational management – most often, expressed as financial management. Our need to base strategy on a detailed plan establishes the expectation that following – or at least monitoring – the plan represents an effective execution of the business's strategic intent.

A much more useful perspective is to see 'strategy' as leading the business into a future that will allow it to thrive and 'operations' as managing current business activities so that you do them well. Both must include a high-level focus and detailed action to be effective. Both must co-exist and one must inform the other if your business is to evolve.

To move from high-level tactics to strategic implementation, there must be room for the plan to evolve and adapt to operational outcomes and market forces.

What to do?

At its very core, strategy is a future-focused activity. It exists to create the most advantageous environment in which to conduct your business's operational activities – its tactics. Because the future is always in front of us, this should be a perpetual activity that is ongoing – not an event replicated once a year.

It is a journey that has a direction, but no destination.

That direction is informed by a synthesis of the high-level objectives of the business, shifts in the market, changes in what your customers want and the development of your organisation.

Henry Mintzberg in his 1994 book *The Rise and Fall of Strategic Planning* talked about the need to incorporate two elements in our strategy-making. He called these 'deliberate' strategy and 'emergent' strategy.

Deliberate strategy includes those initiatives that are preconceived, require careful planning and have a very specific outcome in mind. This would include capital infrastructure investment or expanding into a new geographic market. These deliberate strategic activities often unfold over an extended period of time and require a clear roadmap to keep them on track. The need to devote capital and organisational resources to these types of projects means that they do need to target very specific long-term benefits and incorporate carefully considered predictions about where the market and the economy are headed.

Emergent strategy includes those actions and activities that are the product of ongoing synthesis of the market and business environment. Mintzberg argues that any business that doesn't include an emergent component in its strategy-making leaves itself dangerously exposed to the rapid pace of technological and competitive change.

Are you ready to change?

» *You understand that the business environment you operate in today changes constantly and you have to learn to work with these market shifts.*

» *You know these forces could easily become allies that your business enlists to help it thrive.*

» *You accept that if you don't have the right foresight you will struggle to survive.*

» *You are ready to do something different from what you are used to.*

» *You are ready to hear why the best way to adapt to this landscape is through the use of projects.*

Think, emerge, project

Twenty-five years on from this work, the pace of change has only increased and the potential impacts of this change have increased in both scope and magnitude.

> It is even more important today to incorporate emergent thinking into your strategy-making – in certain industries and markets, it is the single most important part of an effective strategic approach.

An effective emergent approach also requires that you turn what is happening in the market, what is happening within your business and what your ongoing operational activities are telling you about potential business opportunities into action – strategic activities, not just operational reactions to emerging data. Many of these strategic activities will start preparing the business for a future shift in approach or focus. Still others will be experiments to test hypotheses about where business opportunities might lie.

When done well, these emergent strategic activities are used in concert with your deliberate strategic work. This means informing the business which major strategic initiatives represent the best investments, maximising their chance of success by testing them in a controlled manner before committing large-scale, and gaining the broadest possible perspective from your people on the best means of implementing them.

These emergent projects serve as forward scouts for your broader business direction - both in the market and with your people. By making strategy a progressive and adaptive process that involves your people, you signal new directions and strategic priorities in the workplace before highly uncertain major initiatives.

Remember, today's most effective strategy-making is not about defeating the competition that you know, but about preparing and adapting your business for the changes on the horizon.

You must make your people a part of the shift, not one of the things you need to shift.

Businesses no longer resemble large machines in which your people are merely cogs - cogs that just need to know which way to turn, possessing no more strategy than knowing they are meant to mesh with adjacent cogs. Repetitious and routine work is rapidly being replaced by automation and artificial intelligence.

Ever-greater percentages of our workforce are now expected to engage their skills, experience and knowledge to undertake the operational activities of the business and solve day-to-day business problems.

Even in so-called blue-collar industries, much of the front-line workforce doesn't merely show up to work every day to do the tasks they're told to in much the same way as they've always done them. They are now knowledge workers who are expected to think about the effectiveness of their work and adapt it as the operational situation changes. They are expected to assess those operational situations in a myriad of complex ways that the 1920s automotive or steel mill worker was not.

The modern enterprise is more akin to a large, complex biological organism whose interdependencies and interactions are understood far better by the people within it than by the brain that supposedly controls it.

The challenge for you as a leader is to help improve the connectedness of this complex organism – to connect your organisational neuro-pathways between the knowledge and experience at the edge of the organisation and the strategic thinking that will determine where it is headed. This is where truly effective strategy-making begins.

Projectify points

1. Business strategy has evolved out of military tradition to be a very static, analytical activity disconnected from operations and inaccessible to the workforce. It lacks the action and activity that would bring it to life.

2. These days, we intend strategy to be the common thread that holds a business together, but too often this thread breaks under the strains of the constantly shifting environment.

3. Our analytical approach to strategy means that we often mistake 'now-focused' high-level operational activities for the 'future-focused' work of truly effective strategy-making – both strategy and ongoing operations have high-level and detailed elements but should not be confused with each other.

4. It is more important than ever to ensure your strategy has both deliberate and emergent strategic elements if you are to adapt to the highly dynamic world within which your business must operate, or to respond to the uncertainty that lies ahead.

5. The modern enterprise is more akin to a large, complex biological organism whose interdependencies and interactions are understood far better by the people within it than by the brain that supposedly controls it.

6. To ensure you constantly evolve toward a brighter future, you must make your people a part of the shift, not one of the things that you need to shift.

3

A two-way bridge

'Imagine if your workplace culture was the engine room of strategic activity rather than the resistance you are trying to manage.'

Adopting a project-led approach to strategy can achieve what this statement proposes. The transformation of IBM under the guidance of Lou Gerstner in the 1990s is a perfect example of this.

When Lou Gerstner took over IBM in 1993, it had just posted the largest annual loss in its history (US$8 billion). During the 1980s, a strategic plan targeting $100 billion in top-line revenue saw the company invest heavily in infrastructure and people. By the 1990s, they were using outdated organisational transformation approaches and trying to stay rooted in their 'core business' to stem a tide of over-capitalisation, fierce competitive pressures, a shifting computer market, declining customer loyalty and a demoralised workforce (things, quite frankly, had all gone to shit).

Gerstner put a strong focus on doing things differently.

He applied a nimbler, more adaptive approach and empowered IBM's people by bringing them together as project-based teams.

From the outset, Gerstner eschewed strategic plan development in favour of decisive, immediate action. In 1994, shortly after taking over the CEO role, he famously said, 'The last thing IBM needs right now is a vision.'

This wasn't to say that Gerstner didn't have a strategic direction for the organisation. He knew that IBM's strength lay in its diversity and broad computing experience. He recognised that every industry needed an integrator. He believed that IT customers would value a business that could bring the disparate parts of technology together to deliver business outcomes. He knew he needed to mobilise that diversity: not as a means of balancing divisional profit and loss, but as a means of delivering comprehensive solutions to IBM's clients.

One of Gerstner's first moves as a new CEO was to quash a plan already underway to break IBM into a series of smaller autonomous operating units, each with its own identity and direction. He called it 'the most important decision I ever made - not just at IBM, but in my entire business career.'

It was a perfect example of strategic execution – a short, sharp project to prepare the business for the future that its new CEO was looking to achieve.

In this case, it was a project to undo a large transformational change.

A project mindset

To fully transform his strategic insights into operational reality, Gerstner recognised that the long game at IBM was to turn around a toxic, internally competitive culture that had lost sight of customers and the marketplace.

Divisions were actively competing against each other, both within the organisation and out in the marketplace. The drive to meet strategic revenue targets meant the company had broken trust with its customers – seeing them more as sources of sales growth rather than business partners. Not exactly the ideal environment for offering customers a comprehensive, full-service technology solution.

So Gerstner set about shaping IBM for a new and very different future – first, in the relationship the business had with its people; and second, in the promise it was making to its customers.

Gerstner recognised that this was an evolutionary process. In *Who Says Elephants Can't Dance?* he says:

> Changing the attitude and behavior of thousands of people is very, very hard to accomplish. You can't simply give a couple of speeches or write a new credo for the company and declare that a new culture has taken hold. You can't mandate it, can't engineer it. What you can do is create the conditions for transformation, provide incentives for change.

Nearly all of the projects he put in place were made up of cross-functional teams intentionally designed to break down divisional and functional silos. The earliest of these projects was to create a more solid financial footing for the company so that it had a future to adapt to. This included improvements to the cost-pricing structure of its mainframe computing business, which had become grossly over-priced in an ever-more competitive market.

His medium-term focus was built around projects that developed organisational capability for the new IBM. His teams were tasked with creating projects partnering with competitors to deliver more robust technology solutions – an absolute no-go zone for the IBM of the past. A cross-business team worked to create a compensation structure tied to overall organisational performance, rather than business unit performance. This system rewarded speed to market and the reliability with which people met their commitments over sales or revenue targets and KPIs – the exact qualities that a nimbler organisation would require.

Gerstner continued to focus on projects and used this project mindset to move IBM toward a new future – a new incarnation – over the next decade. 'Big Blue' went from a US$8 billion loss in 1993 to an US$8 billion annual profit in 2001.

More importantly, IBM transformed its two most important relationships – the one with its people and the one with its customers.

Projectifying your strategic activities is the most effective means of evolving your organisation at the pace of the change you are trying to respond to.

At the heart of this evolution is the connection that a project mindset creates between who you want to be in your customers' eyes and who you are on a daily basis. It allows you to trade management 'busyness' for leadership attention by better leveraging the capabilities and customer-centric knowledge of your people.

By developing and selecting the right strategic projects, you create the ability to respond to change in a rapid and targeted way. You unlock opportunities in a manner that maximises the experience for your customers and minimises the risk and impact to your current operations.

Projectify now

- ***Projects shift your mindset from results to action.***
  They create a means of moving the future into the day-to-day. They test strategic intent against operational reality.

- ***Projects create a bridge between the business and your people.***
  This two-way bridge allows them to be part of the strategic change you're trying to make, and allows you as the business leader to tap the capabilities and knowledge of your people to inform and operationalise your strategy.

- ***Projects are the ideal structure to connect a problem with the solution and ideas with execution.***
  Making a project mindset part of your day-to-day operational reality is a way of creating a workplace where value is continuously created and enhanced. It brings strategy out of the annual planning cycle and into emergent activity – continuously testing and challenging the strategic direction.

- ***An effective project mindset is one that moves away from large transformational change in favour of a steady stream of smaller adaptive projects.***
  Targeted projects allow you to touch multiple areas of the business in a strategic way much more quickly. Making them smaller and shorter increases the likelihood of the project team reaching a clear outcome. This allows you to progressively shape the business for the future it seeks to create.

Playing to win

Research has consistently shown that organisations with performance-based cultural traits and an engaged workforce out-grow, out-perform and outlast other businesses. Gallup's 2013 Employee Engagement Assessment showed that companies in the top quartile in engagement out-performed companies in the bottom quartile by 10% on customer ratings, 21% in productivity and 22% in profitability.

Similarly, Aon Hewitt's 2014 Engagement Report found some dramatic differences between companies in the top and bottom quartiles for engagement when comparing their performance against the average for sales growth (4% above versus 1% below), operating margin (2% above versus 3% below) and shareholder return (4% above versus 8% below).

This shows that projects are a team game. The right projects create an opportunity for the business to not only engage its employees in a powerful way, but to direct that engagement towards work that will make the business stronger.

The 'project game' is won or lost based on how well the team plays toward a common goal.

Projects are a two-way bridge connecting an organisation's leaders with its people, giving employees the power to make a meaningful difference to the business they serve.

Focused leadership is required to move a project from a great idea that your team never has time to get started on (or gets done under pressure at the last minute) to a key strategic activity that builds new capabilities and improves business.

Figure 3.1 shows how a shift in leadership focus can generate greater returns on the investment your organisation makes in projects, which then increase the value to your business.

Figure 3.1: The adaptive project continuum

	ROI	Focus	Business Value	Adaptive
4	50 to 1	Bandwidth	Thriving	↑
3	10 to 1	Capability	Innovating	
2	5 to 1	Triage	Improving	
1	less than 1 to 1	Starting	Recovering	↓ Reactive

Starting

Many leaders focus only on **starting** because they have a continuous range of improvement projects that either never get off the ground or languish in an incomplete state as teams struggle to find time away from their 'day jobs' to finish them. Some of the most aspirational don't get traction because it never seems to be the right time.

Many organisations feel that by starting a lot of projects the law of averages will mean that they'll finish more projects. Even when this is true, it doesn't mean that you'll complete the right projects – those most strategically important to the business."

The most critical projects will often get done under the pressure of deadlines or crisis, but fail to produce particularly innovative or cost-effective outcomes. As a result, the business improvement initiatives only provide **recovery** and rarely provide a positive return on investment.

Triage

To move above the line and begin getting a positive return from your projects you need to treat them like investments. Wise investment comes from selecting good projects – projects that matter. A **triage focus** means you select the best project investments and eliminate those that are not a high-value use of your time, energy and capital – at least not today.

The criteria for assessing your projects are strategic value and capacity. You prioritise projects according to their criticality to your strategic objectives, then select the highest priority projects to work on, based on your organisational capacity to give them undivided attention.

Triage is not an event – it's a process. The power of projectifying your strategic activities lies in the continuous process of assessing your project portfolio and adjusting the projects it includes, based on current priorities and emerging opportunities. Continuously making good project investments allows you to become an **improving** business.

Capability

Once your project selection is sound and you start to establish a project mindset, you begin growing your organisational 'project muscle' – building **capability**.

The key skills, practices and systems required to build this type of capability are focused on building a performance culture that generates project team autonomy, embraces the project environment as a place to explore ideas and ensures that day-to-day project activities remain focused on the strategic outcome. Of utmost importance is the capability to turn project activities into operational results for the business.

Much of this capability development responds best to a 'learn by doing' approach, so your projects not only generate strategic improvements, they also expand your creativity, increase engagement and improve performance. As you get better at doing projects, your projects will begin to produce **innovative** results that will give your business an advantage over the competition.

Bandwidth

With a skilful and effective project approach established, you can expand the **bandwidth** of your projects. As your projects begin to unleash more of your team's capability in a self-directed manner and relieve the business's leadership of many of the low-value activities, you create time for the 'new'.

You give leaders the ability to lead. The bandwidth to initiate and support projects: not simply in response to disruptive influences, but actually creating the disruption that the market and your competitors are responding to. You create the organisational time and attention for translating strategic insight into action and activity, as well as using strategic activity better to create new strategic insight.

Your employees won't need to be made to buy into your projects – they will become the source of them. When you move into this phase you become a **thriving** organisation that rewards its shareholders and delights its customers in any business climate because you'll see opportunity everywhere.

An ongoing evolution

As you get better at adopting these leadership focuses, you start to move from a world where your strategy is restarted every year to one where the strategic direction is re-visited and reset every year, but strategic execution is always ongoing through your projects.

Your leadership can focus on the future state you want to move towards, rather than managing the day-to-day activity of strategic execution.

By projectifying strategic activities, we don't just step through the project continuum sequentially, we progress the levels simultaneously. We create layers (triaging our strategic activities, building capability and creating bandwidth) that get transformed into business value at different rates.

This project-based approach enables three streams of development to occur simultaneously:

1. Business improvement.
2. Capability development.
3. Culture development.

It has layers rather than steps – it is multi-dimensional. This not only makes you more nimble and quicker to adapt, it allows each stream of development to be more effective. Your capability development has application and is driving strategic improvement. Your cultural development is enhanced because you give your people something to be engaged in and meaningful progress to be motivated by.

When strategic execution (through projects) starts to become part of your operational framework and part of what people see as their day-to-day roles, the following starts to happen:

» The organisation's work becomes better connected to your business purpose and has forward momentum, rather than being mired in faithfully reproducing the best of the past.

» You add depth to your strategic synthesis – the information that informs your strategic thinking and direction. Improvement projects undertaken by the people on the frontline of creating customer value inform strategic direction in ways that marketing analysis never can.

» You begin to leverage the capabilities and diversity of skills and experience across your entire organisation to drive strategic development. Done well, your workplace culture becomes the engine room of strategic activity, rather than the resistance you are trying to manage.

When you break
the strategic journey
into projects,
you get better
at focusing people's
time and leveraging
their attention,
to create space for
the strategy to evolve.

Projectify points

1. Projects allow you to tackle the greatest challenges to strategic execution – time and attention. They leverage the capacity of your entire organisation to drive strategy, not just the leadership team's capacity.

2. Projects are a two-way bridge connecting leaders with their organisation's people, and giving employees the power to make a meaningful difference to the business they serve.

3. By projectifying strategic activities, we don't just step through the project continuum sequentially – we progress the development levels simultaneously, creating a nimbler, more adaptive organisation.

4. We create layers (triaging our strategic activities, building capability and creating bandwidth) that get transformed into business value at different rates – each layer strengthens and enhances the other developmental layers.

5. By breaking the strategic journey into a series of steps, you're not only better utilising your people's time and attention, you're also creating space for the strategy to evolve based on strategic activity and the changing business environment.

PART II
EXECUTION

So now you know that the dynamic times we live in are no place for post-Industrial Revolution management practices. You appreciate the need to stay nimble and constantly adapt your business to the environment in which it operates and the ever-changing expectations of your customers.

If you've read this far, you are probably intrigued by the idea of projectifying your strategic activity – that this approach might shift you from the high-stakes, high-risk game of organisational transformation to one where your business moves at the speed of the change you're trying to keep pace with.

Now the questions start to come, the enormity of the task starts to settle in. How do I instil a project mindset across my organisation? Where do I start? Is it really something I can make sustainable and self-perpetuating? Can I really create enough space in my people's already busy world to get them to see beyond the day-to-day and glance toward the horizon?

It is here that many business leaders start to think that traditional approaches look pretty good; that the default approach is attractive. After all, how can you be criticised for doing what has been done for over a century – for believing that what has gotten you to where you are will continue to take the business to where you want to go?

But as we've seen, this approach is no longer just short-sighted; it actually makes you blind to the disruption just around the corner or the competitor who's doing exactly what you do for cheaper. At best, it can put you in a slow decline. At worst, it can find you in a race to the bottom – commoditised in a world that regularly punishes commodity products and services.

Certainly, building strategic activity into your organisation's operational routine takes effort. It requires a shift in thinking

– both for yourself and your enterprise. But the beauty of projectifying this shift is that it happens progressively – it doesn't have to turn your operational world upside down. It doesn't need to consume all the leadership bandwidth of your management team.

To transform your strategic endeavours from a process of perpetual planning to one of adaptation and growth, you need to start by understanding there are three key influences on strategic performance, as shown in Figure II:

1. **Empower your team** – the way you operationalise your business activities, the way your people work together.
2. **Follow the project framework** – your business routines, practices and systems that enable strategic work to happen in a structured and continuous way.
3. **Share your purpose** – the level alignment of the entire organisation on what represents value for the business, for its customers and for the people in the business.

Figure II: Influences on strategic performance

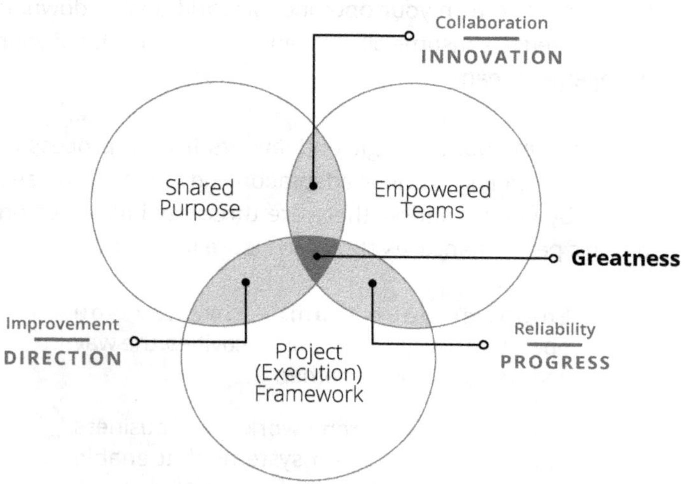

Over the next three chapters, we'll discuss exactly how to maximise each of these influences in a manner that makes strategy an ongoing, sustainable part of your business activity and allows you to constantly evolve into the organisation that you aspire to be.

4

Empower your team

When General Stanley McChrystal took over as commander of the Joint Special Operations Task Force in Iraq in 2003, the joint allied forces were effectively losing the war to a nimbler and more technologically savvy enemy.

Bureaucracy, outdated command and control approaches and a lack of overall integration were constantly limiting their ability to successfully complete missions – the key performance outcome for any 'active' military organisation.

With an average of five missions completed per day, General McChrystal recognised that the traditional military operational model was failing them. The joint force comprised several nations, each with different branches of the military, with each military branch made up of multiple divisions, departments and command centres, creating a mind-blowing organisational structure and tortuous channels of communications. Conventional military command and control leadership was incapable of breaking down the silos and red tape that would allow front-line troops to function as one – or, for that matter, function at all.

Whenever a field force required intelligence on a target, the information was hopelessly out of date by the time it arrived. Ground troops that needed air or logistical support were constantly thwarted when that support was allocated elsewhere or made available only after the mission window had passed.

McChrystal recognised that despite their superiority in numbers and military capability, to effectively turn the tide of the war against Al Qaeda the allies needed to be more like their enemy – they needed to become more operationally nimble and adaptive by eschewing command and control operations in favour of a decentralised operational approach. To do that the task force needed to break down silos, move decision-making as close to the action as possible and bring a collective approach to strategic development. This meant shortening and opening the communication pathways between front-line teams. Ultimately, it meant discarding several centuries of traditional wisdom on organising and leading a military for a new way of conducting military operations.

McChrystal moved the task force from a traditional hierarchal structure to a networked operational model that he calls a 'Team of Teams'. Each of these teams was modelled on the best practices of the smallest units that carried out their military function. To a significant extent, they were also cross-disciplinary so that they could be as self-sufficient as practicable. The joint central command became a team that sat at the centre of the network (rather than on top of it!) whose role was to support and enable the other operational teams as well as establish the strategic direction.

To ensure this remade networked organisation worked, the task force came together in a virtual meeting every day – this included several thousand people from multiple nations across three continents. The focus of these daily discussions was creating transparent inter-team communication – sharing learning and intelligence, coordinating mission activity and making requests for support and assistance. In the early days, this level of interaction met with tremendous resistance and limited active participation. However, General McChrystal persisted with what the leadership called 'forced fun' until it finally started to have an impact on their effectiveness as a military force.

As this effectiveness took hold, mission performance began to improve. First, to between 10 and 20 missions completed per day; then, from 50 to 60 missions per day until a final average of over 140 missions per day when General McChrystal left the joint command in 2010. The joint task force went from a lumbering military dinosaur to a faster, flatter, more flexible organisation that was able to beat back Al Qaeda.

> This is a dramatic example of how powerful shifts in thinking about the way that you operationalise your team can be when faced with a highly dynamic and non-traditional business environment.

Let's face it, there could be no more dynamic or non-traditional environment than the war in the Middle East during the mid- to late 2000s. The example is all the more poignant because it took place in the kind of hierarchical, command-and-control military organisation that most of today's business operations are modelled after. General McChrystal and his team showed that even the largest, most diverse and traditional organisations can be shaped to be more adaptable – to keep pace in a world that moves quickly and can strike out of the shadows at any time.

In order to understand how this example relates to your business and the way that you shape your teams for strategic effectiveness, we need to take it apart and put it back together again. We need to explore how the team environment can affect your people's engagement and motivation and how levels of engagement and motivation can influence the effectiveness of your team.

Command, control and creativity (or lack thereof)

Many organisations still view their businesses as complicated machines and the people in them as components of the overall machinery.

Central to this is the belief that a good manager needs to keep a firm hand on the controls to make the machine run smoothly, so that the team remains under control.

I often hear senior managers talk about the need to 'drive the team' in order to get positive results. While many contemporary management philosophies are advancing the need for organisations to engage with their employees, the command and control approach to worker motivation persists in many organisations today.

This command and control methodology dates back to Frederick Taylor's Scientific Management movement. One of Taylor's most enduring legacies is the modern business operational model, which has remained largely unchanged for 120 years. This model is founded on the belief that businesses are made up of thinkers and doers.

Just as in military-style hierarchies that have existed for centuries, the thinkers are situated at the top of the organisation and are called 'managers', while the doers – the 'workers' – are part of a large machine directed by these managers. Managers tell the workers what results are expected, then measure these results and tell the workers whether they are meeting expectations.

The command and control operational approach has a number of issues that can adversely affect performance:

1. Strategic direction is disconnected from where work actually gets done because it has passed through many hands (i.e., perspectives) before reaching the working level.
2. The silos formed by this approach mean that work tends to be optimised for the individual's or the work group's objectives, rather than for the organisation as a whole.
3. Communication between individuals and work groups usually goes up through the chain of command then back down again – how far up depends on the magnitude of the issue being coordinated.
4. There is little opportunity to take advantage of the collective experience and expertise at the edges of the organisation, because it is not part of the flow of information and knowledge.
5. There is also a tendency for direction to be a reaction to negative results rather than proactively seeking to create opportunity. This means you're constantly working 'below the line' rather actively seeking to rise above it.

Each of the above issues is an impediment to effective collaboration, because it strips away the power of a team to work together for the organisation's greater good.

Is your workplace engaged and motivated in a way that allows you to tap into your people's creativity, their dedication and their day-to-day connection with both your customers and the operational environment that serves them?

There is nothing wrong with hierarchies for reporting and for the care and feeding of your staff. Creating common groups for different types of expertise allows for effective professional development and appropriate allocation of the technical workload. However, for strategic activities – for project work – it is much more effective to form cross-functional teams pooling diverse capabilities and experiences.

This shortens communication pathways and gives the team access to the expertise they need to successfully carry out their project work with a minimum of external interfaces.

Circles, not triangles

In his TEDxAuckland presentation, corporate anthropologist Michael Henderson suggests that if you ask most people in a business environment to describe their organisation as a geometric shape, the overwhelming majority will say it is like a triangle sitting on its base with the leader at the apex. On the other hand, if the same question is asked about a tribal culture, it will most often be described as circular with the leader in the centre. This distinction is important when we begin to consider the structural and operational attributes of an effective team (not simply how you draw your org chart).

Traditionally, businesses have a very hierarchical or 'triangular' operational model – the person at the apex of the triangle directs those below them. Furthermore, like a set of Russian matryoshka dolls, there are usually triangles within triangles with ever-smaller work groups being directed by the role at the apex.

This might be fine as a reporting hierarchy, but it significantly limits the effectiveness of teams. It makes front-line staff too disconnected from their organisational purpose and it inhibits individuals from coming together to pool their knowledge and experience for the greater good of the organisation.

A much more effective team operational model is one where the planning and control of the work is in the hands of the people most responsible for doing the work.

In this distributed planning and control approach – this tribal approach – to operational structure, leadership is situated at the centre of the organisation providing support and strategic guidance to the teams responsible for doing the work, who are situated at the edge of the organisation. Ideas, expertise and requests for things that sustain the work flow inwards, adding value to the business and enabling the business's leadership to enhance the quality of their support and direction.

Michael Henderson has observed that, unlike corporate environments where 20% of the people do 80% of the work, tribal environments have 90% of the people doing 100% of the work. Or, as in the case of the joint forces in the Middle East during the 2000s, you can go from losing the war to winning it.

By moving from a centralised command and control team structure to a distributed planning and control operational model, you create a culture where effective collaboration is the driver behind your performance results.

To operationalise your strategic activities and begin to shape an effective collaborative culture, you want to bring your people together in cross-functional teams that are integrated across reporting lines so that they have all the skills and perspectives at their disposal to do the work effectively and autonomously. The team should be made up of people most familiar with the area of the business you want to evolve strategically, and should include not only staff who work in the area that you're looking to improve or develop but also those who will be impacted by the project.

These work teams – or project teams, in the case of strategic activities – should be responsible for the planning and decision-making around how their work gets done on a day-to-day basis. They're responsible for how problems will be solved and where capacity will be allocated. Of utmost importance, they're responsible for making commitments to each other for the tasks they will complete to meet the team's objectives.

The executive leadership then has responsibility for supporting and enabling the project teams as they go about their project work. More than ever, support is becoming an essential leadership quality if a business is looking for its people to be the driving force behind its success. In his book *The New Rules of Management*, Peter Cook describes four different support roles:

1. **Champions** – those who advocate for and sing the praises of the project team.
2. **Advisors** – those who lend their experience and expertise through advice and mentorship.
3. **Assistance** – support that directly or indirectly assists the team in carrying out project activities.
4. **Buddies** – peers, colleagues or friends who provide encouragement and a sounding board.

As a business leader, you're well placed to have a hand in the first three of these roles. To do this, you need to be connected to the project team and their ongoing activities. This connection is best done through sponsorship rather than oversight. This allows you to influence positive project outcomes in a much more effective way than taking on the day-to-day role of managing them.

Enabling these activities includes creating a framework for setting and re-setting the strategic direction and, as a result, the strategic priorities. It includes providing the leadership necessary to identify, prioritise and initiate a steady stream of strategic projects in line with that framework. It also includes establishing a structured approach for the way the team executes their projects and helping to build understanding and capability around that approach.

When your strategic organisation is operationalised in this way, you're asking your employees to partner with you to shape an exceptionally engaging and motivating workplace. You'll create teams with the diverse capabilities and resources to effectively collaborate on solutions to the business's most pressing problems and answers to its most intriguing questions. As a business, you'll form a tribe that works collaboratively to shape a future where you delight your customers and deliver outstanding results for your shareholders.

Practical project tip

1. *Create work teams that are cross-functional and organisationally integrated so that they encompass all the disciplines required to perform the work.*

2. *Populate these teams with the people most responsible for performing the work on a day-to-day basis – the last planners. Give these teams responsibility for planning and controlling the work in a systematic, structured way that serves the overall delivery strategy and overarching project objectives.*

3. *Make the project sponsorship responsible for establishing a structured approach for managing the project work, and ensuring discipline and commitment to that approach. They are also responsible for driving continuous improvement – but done through a process of co-creation with the team.*

Carrots and sticks

Historically, to get people doing what we want them to do when we want them to do it, we reward desirable behaviour and punish unwanted behaviour.

This 'carrot and stick' approach to motivation is built on a metaphor that equates a team of humans with a team of horses – dangle a bunch of carrots in the direction that you hope to lead them and biological drivers will compel them to follow; whack them with a sharp stick when they step out of line and in line they will stay.

But is it effective?

Studies have shown that external incentives and fear of punishment rank quite low as motivators for today's workforce and are, in fact, detrimental in the long run where the work is non-routine and knowledge-based.

Economists, behavioural scientists and psychologists have all found that although these external motivators may appear to create short-term improvement, the results are almost always far short of what an engaged and intrinsically motivated team can achieve.

These studies have shown that 'intrinsic' motivation can be far more powerful than external (or 'extrinsic', as researchers describe it) motivation for businesses and business endeavours that require creativity and problem-solving. In his book *Drive: The Surprising Truth About What Motivates Us*, Daniel H. Pink brings together the findings from 40 years of behavioural research on motivation – specifically, he makes the case for the long-term power of intrinsic motivation in today's workplace. He explains how Type I behaviour – behaviour driven by internal desires rather than external ones – is the means to get your people's best work.

Pink says that to engage a team's intrinsic motivation, you must tap into three elements that foster this Type I behaviour:

1. **Purpose** – our innate need for connectedness: being part of something larger than ourselves.
2. **Autonomy** – our need for self-determination and the ability to direct our own lives.
3. **Mastery** – our desire to learn, grow and create in the work that we do.

Dr. Teresa Amabile, of Harvard Business School, brings a twist to this construction of intrinsic motivation. In 15 years of research examining psychology and performance of people doing complex work inside businesses, she found a strong correlation between intrinsic motivation and creativity, engagement and performance – all very desirable Type I behaviours for future-focused work.

In one multi-year study, Dr. Amabile examined the daily diaries of hundreds of workers to determine what motivational forces were in play when they were delivering their best creative and productive performance. She found that of the five most commonly identified motivational factors (recognition, incentives, interpersonal support, progress and clear goals), 'progress' was the number one performance motivator for a knowledge-based workforce.

Her research also found that it wasn't just any progress that elicited a worker's creatively engaged best. Even small wins could have a significant motivational impact if the work was meaningful – if it sat within a larger context. In addition, these small wins on meaningful work drove a desire toward further progress – to get more small wins. This creates, as Dr. Amabile puts it, 'an upward spiral of creativity, engagement and performance.' It also makes progress a fourth element for fostering Type I behaviour.

Interestingly, when Dr. Amabile conducted a separate survey of 600 managers from dozens of companies and asked them to rank the impacts of the five key motivational factors on employee performance, they ranked 'progress' last. Presumably these managers believed that without a healthy supply of carrots and a firm hand on the reins, the horses would wander into the paddock and start munching clover at the first opportunity.

Using projects helps organisations move beyond ineffective carrot-and-stick management practices and creates workplaces that bring out the very best in their people.

Building bridges

Projectifying your strategic execution is not only the bridge to a new way of leading your business to the future that you aspire to, but it also creates fertile ground for the growth of intrinsically motivated and engaged teams.

As we see from the research, once your people are intrinsically motivated by and engaged in the business's strategic endeavours they are much more likely to bring creativity to those endeavours and progress them in a productive manner. How good would that be!

So how do you build this bridge? How do you create strategic projects that intrinsically motivate the teams that undertake them?

The answer lies in paying careful attention to the four elements that elicit Type I behaviours. This means framing your strategic projects and shaping your project teams so that you draw out and amplify these four key elements.

1. Purpose

By connecting your desired project outcomes to your higher-level strategic objectives and being clear about each project's priority in the strategic landscape, you attach meaning to the work that the team is undertaking. They can see how their project work is part of something larger. By giving the project team the freedom to define their own vision of how these outcomes might manifest themselves as operational or customer experiences, you further reinforce their connection to this strategic purpose. (We'll explore this in depth in Chapter 6.)

2. Autonomy

To empower a project team, autonomy needs to take the form of self-direction and freedom. The team needs to be able to self-determine their approach to solving the problem or testing the hypothesis that the project sets out to address. They need to be given the responsibility for planning and executing the work in ways they believe best deliver the target outcome. For the future-focused work of strategy-making, they need to be given the freedom to fail – this empowers them to test new ideas and explore the boundaries of what's possible.

There is much debate on whether the most effective improvement teams are self-managed (i.e., everyone takes responsibility for managing themselves) or whether it is best to have a designated leader. I fall on the side of assigning a project leader, based on my own experiences, but many organisations have had tremendous success with self-managed teams. One thing is certain – a leader needs to be a part of the team, at its centre, not separate from and above it.

You also don't want to mistake autonomy for isolation. Having somewhere to go for assistance and support is – perhaps somewhat counter-intuitively – an essential ingredient for self-direction. Ensuring each project has a leadership sponsor is the most effective means of providing this support. However, leaders must understand that a sponsor's role is connection to the project, not direction of the team. When they are connected they can empower the team by providing the necessary support when needed and championing their efforts with the organisation so the team feels recognised.

3. Mastery

If you are to allow your project teams to aspire to mastery – doing their best work and delivering innovative and creative solutions – then they can't spend all their time trying to figure out how to carry out a project. You need to provide them with a project execution framework that gives them structure but is flexible enough to allow them to set their own direction and doesn't stifle creativity. It needs to focus on inter-team reliability – meeting their commitments to each other so that they are in service of one another – and continuous improvement rather than rewarding or punishing short-term results and productivity.

A second element of mastery is active engagement. This means ensuring that team members not only have the tools to succeed, but that individually and collectively they are working on a project that is both deeply satisfying and personally challenging to them. It's important not only to create work environments where these conditions can exist, but to choose team members who feel this way about the work. It is in these conditions that your people will not just do their best work; they will aspire to be their best.

4. Progress

One key attribute of our strategic projects is that they are relatively short-duration, hard-hitting initiatives that target a tangible outcome. The intent of this characteristic is not just to move your strategy forward in a step-wise fashion, but to allow the people undertaking the project work to see progress. If you've been effective at attaching strategic purpose to these projects, then that progress will also be seen as meaningful – not just by the project team involved but by the work groups affected by the project outcomes. When this happens, you not only engender creativity, engagement and performance in the project team that generated the results, but also in the people who were positively impacted by them. Moreover, I have consistently seen that this meaningful progress in one team breeds a desire in the rest of the organisation to be a part of it – to contribute to this progress themselves.

Putting it into place

Before we bring it all together, we need to touch on one more dimension to truly empowering your people to drive your strategic engine.

When Google was looking to create the ultimate team environment, they created 'Project Aristotle' – a multi-faceted analysis on how to get the most out of a team. What they found was that business success lay far from the group of ultra-productive, algorithm-driven technological whiz kids that you might expect of Google.

Instead, the key elements of the best teams lived in the hard-to-measure world of culture and group dynamics: specifically, in what Amy Edmondson, the Harvard researcher who helped everything fall into place, calls psychological safety. She describes it as: 'a sense of confidence that the team will not embarrass, reject or punish someone for speaking up' and a 'team climate characterised by interpersonal trust and mutual respect in which people are comfortable being themselves.'

In his book *Smarter Faster Better: The Secrets of Productivity in Life and Business,* Charles Duhigg provided the following commentary on these findings:

> Project Aristotle is a reminder that when companies try to optimise everything, it's sometimes easy to forget that success is often built on experiences – like emotional interactions and complicated conversations and discussions of who we want to be and how our teammates make us feel – that can't really be optimised.

Edmondson explains that psychological safety is not at the other end of the spectrum from accountability – you don't trade off an open, safe work environment against one where people are accountable for their actions. Psychological safety and motivation/accountability are in fact two separate dimensions of how effectively a team performs. She argues that motivation and accountability are the accelerator you want to push and psychological safety is the brake you want to release. Her research shows that the most effective teams operate at high levels of both motivation/accountability and psychological safety. She calls this the 'learning zone' – the state in which teams develop the most creative and innovative solutions as well as consistently deliver results.

Strategic projects should be a learning environment, not an execution environment.

This was the correlation that allowed things to fall into place for Google on Project Aristotle. They saw that their most important and effective project results came from environments where people felt free to question everything: where they felt empowered to use feeling and intuition as a basis for exploration.

This is precisely the environment you want when undertaking your strategic activities. You want to create a learning zone where everyone feels safe asking questions and exploring long-held truths – the way we do things or what our customers want. You want the people interacting with the 'working parts' of your business to tap into their feelings and intuitions, because they are often the product of operational or customer experiences that will never find their way into your business analytics – until they manifest themselves as a revenue or profit problem. This is how you stop doing what you've always done while hoping for a different result.

Of course, recognising the importance of psychological safety and creating an environment where it exists are two quite different things. Edmondson describes three key steps in helping to create a psychologically safe environment.

1. **Frame your projects as a learning problem** – we need each other's skills and experience if we are to come up with the best solution.
2. **Acknowledge your fallibility** – speak openly about not having all the answers and how not every answer is a good one; start this at the leadership level, but encourage it at every level.
3. **Model curiosity** – ask lots of open questions and be willing to explore ideas.

Today's most successful companies have come to realise that long-term success and the nimbleness to respond to today's dynamic business environment come from the organisation seeing its people as its competitive advantage. They view their employees as solutions to the business's greatest challenges, not as problems they need to fix.

Projectify points

1. Traditionally, to make the business machinery run smoothly, to get people doing what you want them to do when you want them to do it, you reward desirable behaviour and punish unwanted behaviour.

2. To be successful in today's business world, it is not as simple as getting your people to do what you tell them to do in a productive manner. You need ever-greater numbers of your workforce to use their thinking, experience and knowledge in order to drive high performance.

3. By moving from a centralised command and control management approach to a distributed planning and control operational model, you create the groundwork for a culture where effective collaboration is the driver behind performance results.

4. Empowered teams allow the business leadership to focus its limited attention on thinking deeply about strategic direction – synthesising the inputs from the environment, customers and strategic projects – then supporting and enabling the execution of that strategy.

5. When you move beyond what traditional practice has taught us about motivating and engaging people, you can use projects to tap into four powerful components of workplace motivation: purpose, autonomy, mastery, progress.

---

6. When you bring together an operational environment that actively fosters collaboration, a project environment that intrinsically motivates and engages your people, and a psychological environment in which people feel safe to test boundaries and express their most creative thoughts, you create cultural layers that feed into and amplify one another; you create an upward spiral of empowerment that drives strategic creativity, engagement, and performance.

5

Follow the project framework

For many businesses, implementing a strategy is like a bike ride to the park a couple of suburbs over. You pull out the bike, check the tyres, do a quick review of the route on the maps app on your phone, then shoot a text to your friends telling them what to bring and 'We'll meet at main pavilion at noon.'

Then off you go expecting to follow the well-marked street signs, gently gliding over the smooth road surface and thinking about how good that barbeque is going to taste once you arrive at your destination. Unfortunately, you find that your maps app has led you astray.

What looked like a well-travelled road was in fact a goat track through the bush – full of potholes and fallen trees.

Even though it had appeared to be a pretty clear path, it was made up of a series of forks, bifurcations and dead-end trails that required careful navigation. What looked like the perfectly level roads familiar to you actually contained steep climbs and white-knuckle descents filled with rocks and roots. The bike, which had seemed fine because the tyres were at the right air pressure, actually had a pretty dodgy drivetrain and required some serious maintenance to keep it moving over this sort of technical terrain.

STRATEGIC PLAN

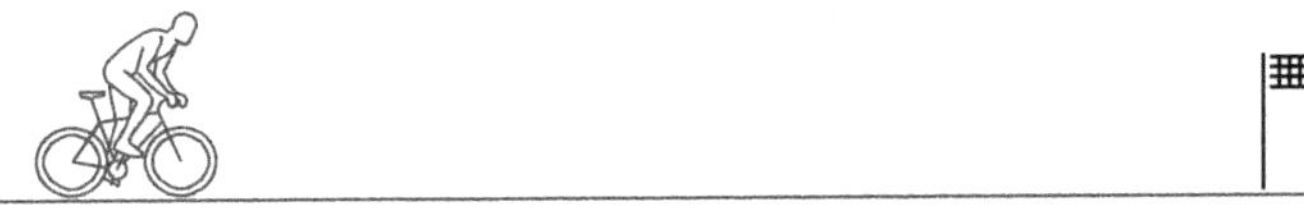

STRATEGIC REALITY

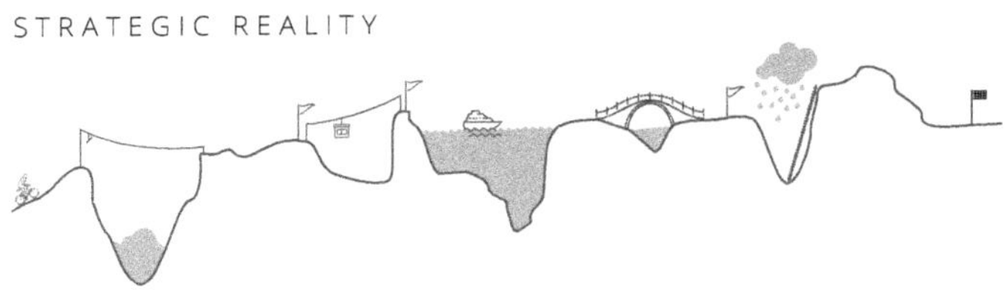

The quick message to your friends about where to meet wasn't as clear as you'd thought and, as a result, people are headed to different pavilions in different parks at different times – and some didn't get the message at all.

If you're fortunate enough to have a business environment that allows you to roll out of the garage along a smoothly-paved path and arrive at your strategic destination just as the rest of your organisation does, then do two things:

1. Express gratitude to the universe for your amazing fortune.
2. Give this book to someone who is not as fortunate as you.

If you're not this fortunate then, luckily you have some important navigational tools at your disposal.

Your strategic intent – your shared organisational purpose – is your compass. It provides the direction for setting your strategic course of action. It then allows you to determine whether the path you're following is taking you where you want to go. (More on this in Chapter 6.)

Your team's skills, experience and intimate knowledge of your customers and the business's operational workings are your route-finding expertise. Use that capability effectively and they will help you avoid many of the cliffs, pitfalls and dead-end gullies that might otherwise cost you time, money and your customers' loyalty. We talked about how to do this in the previous chapter.

In addition to this, to successfully embark on this important journey, you will need an appropriate vehicle for traversing the strategic landscape. You need a bike – a vehicle – that is built for the conditions. You'll need to consistently maintain the gears and brakes so that they work when you need them most. You'll need to build your muscle – your legs and lungs – for the steep climbs and your skills – your teamwork – for the technical descents.

Make no mistake; there will still be times you have to get off the bike and walk around the hard bits. There will be the odd tumble or dead-end trail. There will be flats and breakdowns. But if you accept that this is the trail you're on and that there is a way to ride it that keeps you moving in the right direction while building your strength and capability, then mishaps will be fewer, your ability to read the trail will get better and the riding will get easier.

If you want to be able to traverse the challenging, unknown terrain that most businesses face, you have to be prepared to constantly respond to this terrain.

Your vehicle to vision

In the *Tao Te Ching*, Chinese philosopher Lao Tzu said that a journey of a thousand miles begins with a single step. On a strategic journey, projectifying strategy is the most effective way to take those steps. Through these projects, and a project-mindset, we can take decisive action toward our strategic goals ... one step (or pedal-stroke) at a time.

For example, let's say you have a strategic objective to open up in a new market or undertake a new product or service launch. These initiatives are rarely as simple as putting in place a highly detailed plan then executing it. Their magnitude and complexity often mean they suffer from the inertia of getting underway. They also tend to unfold in a manner far different than originally conceived and require re-planning and adaptation. But if you translate these complex initiatives into a series of smaller projects, not only can you ensure that you're always progressing toward your strategic objective, but also that you have the ability to address challenges and evolving conditions as they arise.

This allows strategic intent to be brought into the present – to be made tangible and connected to a higher strategic purpose. Most importantly, it allows you to consistently and persistently make meaningful strategic progress.

> It turns strategic planning into strategic execution and connects long-term vision to operational reality.

Strategic improvement projects are the advanced scouts of this trail-blazing journey into the unknown. They help you find the path through uncertainty. They are the course corrections you need to find your way out of dead-end trails or around new obstacles suddenly looming before you.

Importantly, they help to find new vistas from which you'll gain insights and discover exciting opportunities.

Five phases to develop a map

The uncertainty of the future business environment is the very reason that you need to be intentional about the way you journey into it.

But where do you begin?

To set out on a journey of this complexity, you need to decide where you're headed – you need a roadmap that your organisation can follow. This includes both the initial steps you'll take on your journey as well as the approach you'll use to refine the roadmap as the journey unfolds.

There are five strategic phases to developing a roadmap of this kind of journey:

1. **Modelling** – set your destination.
2. **Mapping** – identify improvement opportunities.
3. **Exploration** – identify projects.
4. **Execution** – create your project framework.
5. **Roll-out** – prepare your teams.

1. Modelling – set your destination

The first step is to establish and understand your business's operating model, your strategic focus areas and the objectives that you have for them. This modelling activity will explore the threats, opportunities and customer expectations that your strategy needs to address to enhance business value.

An important part of creating a strategic model is to assess the current business situation: what is working effectively, what is not and what your current strategic objectives are. Next, you'll want to use this current situation and an assessment of potential shifts in the business landscape to set your business aspirations – and contrast this with your current business worldview to set your new strategic objectives.

On our metaphorical journey, strategic modelling establishes the destination you are seeking – it creates a beacon for directing all your strategic execution activities.

It provides you with an eyes-wide-open perspective of where you're starting from.

2. Mapping – identify improvement opportunities

Improvement opportunities are the organisational qualities we want to create, improve or amplify – whether operational, product or customer service-focused. In this phase, you map the business's strategic objectives to improvement opportunities by responding to the statement, 'We could achieve that if we did this'.

Be sure not to allow your history and the current conditions to limit your definition of what is possible. Your history should indicate where improvement opportunities exist, but should not limit your goals. Your current situation should indicate the starting point for future improvement and development – not merely define the things you want to keep doing, but better.

The strategic mapping stage is also when you begin to sketch out your strategic roadmap. Imagine it as survey work for establishing the terrain that your strategy must traverse – how will your strategic execution activities unfold and on which frequency? You also want to identify the deliberate strategic initiatives that must be accommodated and how you want to engage with and involve the broader organisation in subsequent phases.

If strategic modelling establishes the destination you are seeking, then strategic mapping does two things:

1. It sets out the initial waypoints to reach that destination.
2. It defines a specific approach to developing the rest of the framework.

3. Exploration – identify projects

The next step is to use your survey of the business landscape to ensure you set off in the best possible direction toward your strategic waypoints.

The best way to explore the business terrain is by identifying projects that will help to realise your improvement opportunities. The strategic improvement projects we're talking about are not big transformational undertakings. They're short-duration, hard-hitting activities that can be carried out by a relatively small cross-functional team. They should target a single specific outcome that delivers strategic value – either on its own or as one phase in a longer program.

In this way, you bring strategic intent into the present – you create specific, tangible activities that are directly connected to your higher strategic objectives.

Strategic improvement projects can take many forms:

» Course corrections or creating opportunities.

» Major changes to the way you do business.

» Incremental operational or process improvements.

» Experiments: hypotheses you want to test to uncover improvement opportunities.

The most effective strategic exploration is done with the people who know the most about the improvement opportunity being pursued – those who are closest to where the element of business value gets produced.

The final, most important part of this step is prioritising the projects you have identified based on their business value. Do this from a range of different perspectives: operational, organisational and customer-centric.

4. Execution – create your project framework

With the strategic improvement projects identified and prioritised, it is time to establish your project portfolio and ready it for execution. Start by triaging the projects according to their priority and your organisation's capacity for strategic activities. You'll recall from Chapter 3 that a key leadership focus is ensuring you only take on those strategic projects that your people have the time and attention to complete.

Once selected, your project teams need to ensure their projects are effectively framed. This means looking at them from four specific perspectives: context, content, people and investment. A cross-functional project team, along with an executive sponsor, should be selected and engaged to begin exploring these perspectives and planning the project.

From a contextual perspective, you want your project teams to be clear about the objectives and outcomes for the project – the improvement opportunity they're meant to serve and the project results that will provide that service. If the project is a single phase of a larger program or the initial exploration of a new business direction, the team should lay out how it fits into this broader context. Given their future-focused nature, they should also have a clear vision of what a successful project would look like – how it would manifest itself in the future that you are trying to create.

The content perspective of the project frame addresses the 'nuts and bolts' of the project – what is the specific scope of activity (the boundaries) - and how that scope will be translated into physical results (what will the team deliver at the conclusion of the project). The content framing should also identify the support and enabling activities that the team will need in place to perform in a powerful way.

The people perspective needs not only to identify the team members necessary to get the best project outcomes. The team also needs to identify the project stakeholders - the people and groups within the organisation who will be impacted by the project or be part of its operational success.

> This ensures the project includes expertise within the team as well as engaging the expertise and expectations of the users and customers the project is meant to serve.

The final perspective for the team to consider is the investment that the business is making in the project. Your strategic projects - and, one could argue, all projects - are investments of capital, time and/or attention. So you'll want to assess the intended return of this investment for the business.

That return might not always be framed in dollar terms; however, there should be a clear line of sight to the business future that the project intends to deliver. With investment, there is almost invariably risk, so any assessment of return must also include a look at the project risks. This includes both the risks that might impact project success as well as the risks that the project might impose on the business.

This second point is an important one, as you don't want your shiny new strategic initiative to have unintended consequences on the successful aspects of your ongoing operations. Think of major IT system roll-outs as the most common example of this risk.

Finally, the project team should agree on the framework for executing the project – how they will work together and interact with the organisation. You want to ensure that the project team is focused on producing exceptional outcomes, not developing project delivery methodologies.

In our metaphorical journey, this phase is where we select and provision the teams that will lead the business on this leg of its strategic journey.

5. Roll-out – prepare your teams

This is the final phase before the strategic journey begins in earnest. The purpose of this phase is to ensure that the journey begins with leadership behaviour that is congruent with strategic intent, and that the project teams are supported and enabled, prepared and committed.

It is also the point at which the strategy should be powerfully communicated so that the entire organisation is accountable for its success. This creates engagement across the business and helps to build cultural momentum around your strategic activities.

It's important
that your strategic
journey commences
with fanfare,
not in quiet stealth.

Map and adapt

An effective strategic roadmap simultaneously improves and adapts the business in three important ways:

1. ***It creates focused strategic activity.***

By selecting high-priority strategic projects, you drive improvement and create strategic progress. Completing projects enables further strategic development – merely starting a large number of strategic initiatives does not. Greater strategic clarity comes on the other side of action. This allows you to make ongoing, well-informed decisions about your strategic direction, rather than simply pursuing a pre-determined strategic plan.

2. ***It makes strategic execution part of your operational fabric.***

The discipline of developing and maintaining a strategic project portfolio allows you to build your project capability. You also make strategic activity a part of your operational routine. Improvement projects are a 'learn by doing' activity, and as this capability develops, your project outcomes move your business from improving to innovating.

3. It creates an environment for a high-performance culture.

Projectifying strategic execution creates an environment where high-performance cultures flourish. It empowers your people to shape their workplace and the business in a meaningful way. The project framework gives them the ability to succeed at these improvement expectations and see strategic progress. This builds strategic bandwidth into the organisation that is greater than its leadership and provides an operational feedback mechanism that allows the business to thrive in any market condition or economic climate.

Make excellence your business

Today, the most successful businesses in the world are project-driven organisations. Google, Apple, Airbnb, Southwest Airlines, 3M and GE all use projects to improve the value they offer their customers and maintain their positions as market leaders. They have moved away from large transformation change projects in favour of a continuous stream of projects that touch multiple areas of the business.

Interestingly, the businesses that use this project-based approach are also among the most desirable places to work. They value the contribution their people can make to the business and actively engage them to drive their success. This allows strategy-making to become personal and meaningful for employees. As a result, their people have become the number one source of their improvement and innovation activities. Very few projects come from senior management.

The first step is to make projectifying your strategic improvement more than an event – make it part of your operational fabric. To do this, you need a process for creating a portfolio of strategic improvement projects that are constantly in motion.

Business excellence comes from using projects to shape a culture that is constantly evolving – not merely from creating a culture that does projects.

Create your project portfolio

Strategic improvement initiatives often fall into one of two camps.

1. *We implement them only when we have a problem to fix. And because we're human and we tend to ignore problems until they become BIG problems, our improvement activities are often reasonably large transformational projects.*

2. *We start as many strategic initiatives as possible in the hope that something will stick – that some percentage of them will reach completion.*

Because these projects are separate from your daily operational routine, your teams are usually lacking the skills and time necessary to implement them successfully. They also often require more time and attention than you have available to devote to them. This means that you start a number of strategic projects and either never finish them or complete what is easiest, not necessarily the most strategically important.

However, meaningful strategic progress comes when you achieve the project outcomes you set out to accomplish. The value of that progress is directly related to the quality of the projects that you do. It is by completing the most important activities that you gain the insights and clarity your business needs to evolve.

Projectifying strategic activities allows you to generate the most valuable strategic progress by creating and maintaining a portfolio of projects – projects that continuously enhance and improve the business. This portfolio consists of a small number of critical or high-value projects that are constantly on the go.

Figure 5.1 shows how these projects are identified, prioritised and then selected for execution: from a macro level to a micro level, outside to inside.

Figure 5.1: Your portfolio of projects

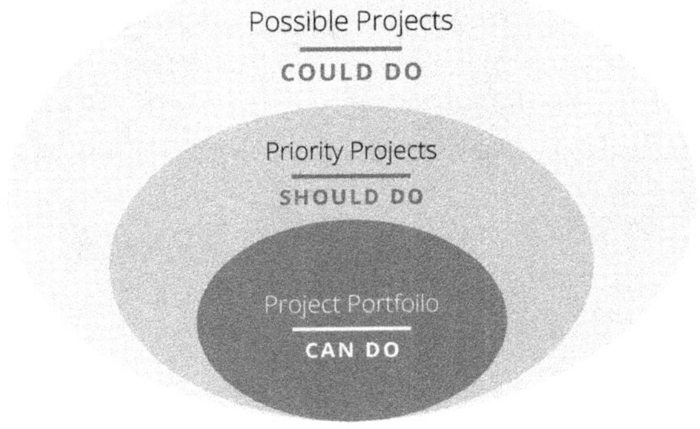

Start by identifying all the 'possible projects': the ones you COULD DO that would allow you to realise or pursue your improvement opportunities. This should be a process of divergence – encouraging identification of the broadest range of project ideas that might provide strategic value.

With this broad range of possible projects identified, you want to initiate a process of convergence – focusing in on the most valuable projects to undertake. You start by prioritising your project ideas to categorise the 'priority projects': the ones that are either critical to business success or have such a high business return that you SHOULD DO them.

In selecting projects to undertake at any given time, you should create a 'project portfolio' consisting of the highest priority projects to which you can devote your undivided attention. These are the projects that you CAN DO: more specifically, the projects that you can complete.

By being intentional about scrutinising and selecting the projects in your portfolio, you maximise the opportunity for successful outcomes on the projects that are the greatest value to your business.

On the road

Once you've launched your strategic execution journey, it has an iterative and perpetual nature that should continuously create forward momentum toward your organisation's best possible future. Your project portfolio is the strategic execution vehicle carrying you forward.

I like to think of your strategic projects as a series of small, tight iterative loops that are constantly rolling forward. All the while, your strategic intent is informing the projects that you should do – via your improvement opportunities – while the projects you do are informing the value that inhabits your strategic thinking.

As discussed earlier, the strategic journey is by no means a smooth one.

Uncertainty and experimentation will take you in directions you didn't anticipate and create dead-ends out of paths that seemed filled with possibility.

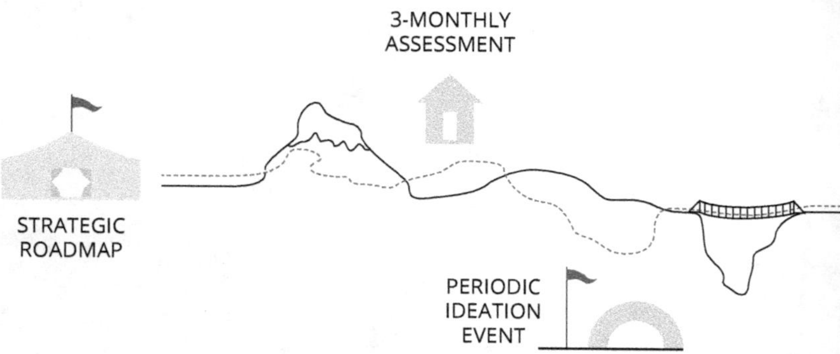

So, along the way your project successes and failures will help define your strategic priorities:

- You use your project results to revisit your improvement opportunities and their priorities.
- You then use those revisited improvement opportunities to refresh your strategic objectives.
- This strategic refresh will suggest new opportunities, which will spawn new project ideas.

Figure 5.2 shows that this perpetual projectifying process exists at two levels – your project portfolio and your strategic objectives. You want to assess and refresh your project portfolio as part of a regular cycle – there is no magic in the timing, but I find a 90-day cycle is the right duration for both maintaining momentum and making meaningful progress. Your strategy should be reset on an annual basis.

Figure 5.2: The perpetual project journey

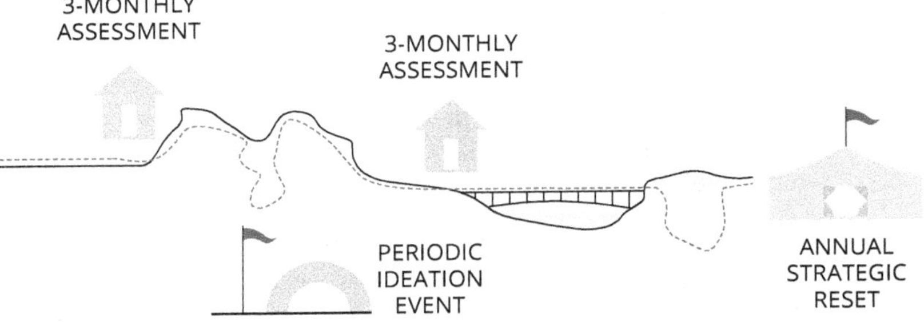

Refreshing and maintaining the project portfolio is a cyclical process that sits within the 90-day project rhythm.

Figure 5.3 shows how this cycle is undertaken in a very intentional manner so you're constantly adjusting the mix of projects in the portfolio to maximise the return on investment.

Figure 5.3: The 90-day project cycle

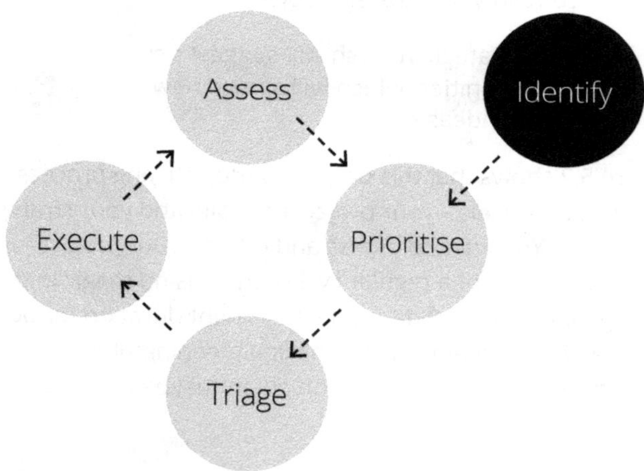

Every 90 days you assess:

- Which projects are succeeding? Can we start implementing them in the operational environment?
- Which ones are failing and proving not to add value? We want to fail quickly and move on to higher value activities.
- Are there emerging issues and opportunities of higher priority that should be the subject of a new project in the portfolio?

Importantly, the process of identifying projects is continuous. Whether through structured ideation events, working sessions with various work groups or individual inspiration, the bucket of possible projects should be continuously filled with high-quality projects if the cycle is to maintain its strategic power.

> You want to create an environment where your people see their ideas captured as soon as they emerge, then actioned as a part of a regular business cycle. This is when they start to contribute pearls of brilliance.

Begin at the end

At the completion of each three-month strategic project period, the cycle starts. You begin by assessing the results of the previous quarter's project performance. This assessment includes a review of project outcomes but it should also incorporate recognition and celebration of success. This creates ritual, which helps to drive culture as well as feed the Progress Principle we have discussed elsewhere.

Finally, your assessment should include a continuous improvement step that takes learnings from the previous quarter's project activities and identifies ways to incorporate them into future projects. These three assessment activities on your past projects create closure, allowing you to shift your focus once again to the future you are trying to create for your business.

The first step into this future should be prioritisation – perhaps better described as re-prioritisation – of your strategic projects. This re-prioritisation should bring together the learnings from your previous project portfolio, the new project ideas that have been identified and any emerging business issues or opportunities that might shift your strategic focus.

The highest priority projects should then be triaged to select your next 90-day strategic portfolio. The projects selected for your portfolio should be executed with the same level of importance as everything else the business does. A project team should be selected with a project leader. The team should be cross-functional and composed of the people that best understand the work that you're trying to improve. The teams are then devoted to those projects and given the time and resources to undertake them successfully.

At the end of the quarterly period, the strategic project cycle begins again.

Make it an annual affair

At the strategic level, the iterative cycle is an annual affair. Once a year, you should reset your strategic roadmap. This means revisiting the five-phase strategic roadmap process – not creating a new strategic plan. This allows you to recognise and celebrate the strategic efforts of the previous year. You then take this strategic progress, any shifts in the business environment and feedback from your customers to re-frame your strategic objectives and reassess your improvement opportunities. This allows you and the organisation to better understand your strategic priorities when developing and selecting your strategic project portfolio.

> Over the course of the year, it is good to have a small number of events that allow you to reconnect with your strategy at a creative level.

This can include development events that specifically look to develop strategic capabilities such as project execution skills, symposiums that enhance technical capabilities to which your staff aren't exposed in their normal operational work or leadership development programs targeted at enhancing your team's ability to lead the type of decentralised organisation that allows projectifying to flourish.

I believe one of the most rewarding creative forums in building a high-performance culture is an ideation event – an event designed to give your people an opportunity to develop the project ideas that will best serve the business's strategic agenda. These may take the form of hackathons or other types of free-form project development days. Alternatively, you can create a more structured forum for specific groups to explore projects that will drive future improvement.

Be strategic; be agile

You might find it surprising that a book written by a former project manager about projectifying your strategy isn't dense with project management techniques and practices – flush with suggestions on establishing PMOs or other organisational structures. This is quite intentional, as nearly 30 years of project management experience has shown me that an over-emphasis on 'managing' projects can blind us to the intended value of those projects.

However, this lack of project management emphasis doesn't mean you can ignore some key practices to maximise the effectiveness of projects. The most important practices ensure that the project work is progressing toward the outcome in an efficient and reliable manner: that the project team is working in a committed and collaborative manner.

The nature of your strategic projects makes them well suited to what are commonly referred to as 'agile' project management practices. Many excellent books explain agile techniques, so I'm not going to cover them extensively here, but I do want to touch on a few particularly important practices when undertaking strategic improvement projects.

- **Charter the team.** *In Chapter 6 we will talk about the importance of creating a sense of shared purpose and common goals at the organisational level. It is equally as important for this shared understanding to exist at the project team level. A project chartering session is designed to create common ground amongst the project team members. The chartering session agenda should:*
    - » *Review target outcomes and vision for the project.*
    - » *Create a shared understanding of the project scope and key deliverables.*
    - » *Define roles and responsibilities of the project team members.*
    - » *Develop a delivery strategy for achieving the project objectives.*
    - » *Develop the delivery framework and operating guidelines.*
    - » *As appropriate to the project, discuss stakeholder communication, risk management and any support or enabling activities required.*

- ***Weekly production meetings.*** *Regular team interactions that establish accountability among team members and create opportunities for collaborative planning are important to maintain momentum and ensure the work is progressing smoothly. A weekly production meeting is the ideal forum for accomplishing this. Each meeting, whether face-to-face or virtual, should include the following elements:*

    - » *Review overall project progress and performance to determine if course correction or outside support is required in order to deliver the project outcome.*

    - » *Plan/re-plan the tasks to be done over the next two to four weeks. This should include identifying any constraints or enabling activities that need to be completed to allow this work to progress.*

    - » *Review the status of the tasks that each team member committed to complete over the previous week.*

    - » *Each team member should commit to the tasks they will complete during coming week.*

- **Daily communication.** *Whether done in real time (synchronous) or virtually (asynchronous), the project team needs an open channel for daily communication so that each member of the team can stay informed on what others are working on or can make requests for support and information. This may take the form of a daily briefing session (sometimes referred to as a 'stand-up meeting'), a digital communication application, or both, depending on the needs and logistics of the organisation. The goal is not for your teams to create a public diary of their individual activities, but to create a forum for sharing information that all members of the team will be interested in, coordinate activities among team members and tap into the collective knowledge of the team to solve problems.*

- **Project retrospective.** *It is important to create a routine for closing out your projects at the end of the quarter – this is what a 'retrospective' is designed to do. This consists of a relatively short meeting (90 minutes should be allocated, but it may take less) with the project team, including the project sponsor, during which you methodically answer the following questions:*

» *Was the project's target outcome met?*

» *Did the project team produce the key deliverables that were identified?*

» *What went well during the project?*

» *What could have been done better?*

» *What lessons have we learned for incorporating into future projects?*

This is an important step for closing out the quarter's strategic execution work. It allows for critical self-assessment of progress against the project's objectives as well as incorporating a continuous improvement feedback loop – both essential elements of a high-performance culture. It is also a prerequisite for kicking off the next project portfolio.

Incorporating these few simple elements into your projects will allow your teams to efficiently and effectively further your strategic agenda and ensure that you maximise return from your project investments.

Projectify points

1. The strategic journey is an uncertain journey where the terrain is constantly shifting and more things lie outside your control than within it.

2. What looks like a well-travelled road is often a goat track running through the bush, full of potholes and fallen trees.

3. Strategic improvement projects are vehicles for managing this terrain, as they turn strategic planning into execution and connect long-term vision into what your people do day-to-day.

4. There are five phases to develop a strategic roadmap:

   i) **Modelling** – set your destination.

   ii) **Mapping** – identify improvement opportunities.

   iii) **Exploration** – identify projects.

   iv) **Execution** – create your project framework.

   v) **Roll-out** – prepare your teams.

5. Once the journey has begun in earnest, you'll want to create a rhythm that consistently and persistently moves your strategic activities forward.

6. Strategic execution is an iterative cycle, during which you assess current projects every 90 days and identify and introduce new ones into the cycle.

7. Your overall strategic direction is an annual cycle where you bring together the results of your projects and an assessment of the business environment to reset your strategic objectives.

6

Share your purpose

In his bestselling book and hugely popular TED talk *Start with Why*, Simon Sinek exposes the difference between leaders and those relatively rare individuals and organisations that lead: the ones who inspire those around them to take action.

Sinek describes a consistent pattern in the way they think, act and communicate that is the exact opposite of the way most leaders and organisations think – because they start with WHY.

Sinek explains that the key to this 'alternative perspective' lies in the Golden Circle and its three concentric rings. In the outer ring is WHAT – the product or service that the company sells or the job function of someone within the enterprise. The WHAT is readily explained and easily understood.

The middle ring is HOW you do WHAT you do. For the customer, this is often couched in terms that differentiate your value or your product from others. For the people in your organisation, the HOW takes the form of process, guidance or training in WHAT you want them to do. The HOW gets a little more conceptual – as well as rarer – when trying to motivate action.

The inner circle is where WHY resides. Sinek suggests that here the secret sauce can be found. Very few people can clearly articulate WHY they do WHAT they do or WHY they want done what they are asking. Sinek further clarifies this point, saying 'When I say WHY, I don't mean to make money – that's a result. By WHY I mean what is your purpose?'

Sinek says that most leaders and organisations look to motivate by using their position or authority to influence and manipulate. They work from outside the Golden Circle toward the centre. They provide a lot of WHAT, perhaps a bit of HOW and very little WHY.

In fact, they often replace a compelling WHY with some external influence – a reward or recognition for successful action and/ or a penalty for failing to act. Sinek says that for most leaders, this is where the motivating driver lies: 'I have told them WHAT to do, I have told them HOW to do it and I have explained the consequences of doing it or not. What more is there to ensuring that it gets done?'

This is not the case for the most effective leaders – they inspire people to act.

Great leaders use inspiration to create a sense of purpose and belonging that makes people perform because they want to, not because it's required.

What sets these leaders apart is that they think, act and communicate from the inside out. These leaders start with WHY, so that the purpose in WHAT an individual does is clear and is articulated in such a way that his or her role is connected to the WHY that the organisation is communicating to its customers. This allows your people to be more engaged in their work – which makes them more productive and more creative. It also better motivates them for the work they do, so they treat their co-workers and your customers better. This creates a workplace where your people are an outward reflection of what you believe as a company and what you want to achieve as a business – which leads to a stronger company and a more loyal customer base.

An important but subtle point that Sinek makes is that when leadership is built not on position but on purpose – on WHY – anyone in your organisation can lead. In this alternative perspective on leadership, a leader is someone who inspires and helps to create greatness in everyone around them. Anyone can lead with their skills. They can lead with their principles and values. They can lead with their determination and commitment. They can lead by supporting others and helping them to be their best.

By understanding your WHY – your business purpose – your people can bring their experiences to bear on strategic activities in a way that has direction, that is leading the business where you want it to go.

From a strategy perspective, a strong sense of WHY gives you the ability to inspire people to take action, serving your strategic interests without having to constantly direct WHAT they do and HOW they do it.

Purpose has power

As we discussed in Chapter 4, a sense of purpose – being part of something larger – is one of the foundational elements of an engaged and internally motivated workforce. Dr. Teresa Amabile's research shows that this sense of purpose is markedly enhanced when your people feel they are contributing to it – making meaningful progress that serves that higher purpose. Her research shows that the highest performing organisations start by giving their people something meaningful to accomplish and respecting their ideas and contributions to the overarching purpose.

She found that this 'Progress Principle' created what she refers to as a 'consistently positive inner work life'. Her research also shows that a positive inner work life is directly correlated with employees being more creative, having higher productivity, being more committed to their work and working more effectively with their fellow employees.

As Dr. Amabile puts it in *The Progress Principle: Using Small Wins to Ignite Joy, Engagement, and Creativity at Work*:

> In light of our results, managers who say—or secretly believe—that employees work better under pressure, uncertainty, unhappiness, or fear are just plain wrong. Negative inner work life has a negative effect on the four dimensions of performance: people are less creative, less productive, less deeply committed to their work, and less collegial to each other when their inner work lives darken.

She goes on to argue that the antidote to this flawed approach to building an effective workplace is ensuring you give your people work that has purpose – that allows them to see the difference they are making. She says that 'management should enrich the lives of the people working inside the organization by enabling them to succeed at work that has real value to their customers, the community, and themselves.'

This isn't merely the fulfilment of some social contract with your employees, as 'work-related psychological benefits for employees translate into performance benefits for the company.'

Dr. Amabile and her research partner Steven Kramer found that the Progress Principle is one of the most important drivers of creativity in the workplace. Your people will have the highest level of engagement, be the most motivated in their jobs and be at their creative best when they have a common set of goals that are tangible and relevant to the business outcomes you hope to achieve.

This makes shared purpose one of the single most important factors in connecting a business to its people. When you combine an understanding of what represents business value with an empowered team, you tap into the depth and breadth of your people's skills and experience in a powerful way. Now employees have common ground to rally around, enabling them to shape how their individual capabilities might contribute to your growth and improvement efforts. You're doing more than simply asking your people to be engaged; you're giving them meaningful work that they can be engaged in. You create the opportunity for them to make a difference – a difference to their own working world, to the people they work with and to the customers that they serve.

When you connect your people's strategic efforts to a higher business purpose, you give them an understanding of the business impact they're having.

You allow them to see that their work is contributing to meaningful progress for the organisation. This motivates them to do more – to keep making progress and adjust their activities to be as meaningful as possible.

This progress drives creativity in solving the business's strategic problems. It also enhances the level of collaboration that exists across your business but, most importantly, exists in the cross-functional project teams you establish to take on these problems.

These inner work-life benefits are not just for your employees; they extend to you as a senior manager as well. As your people become more engaged and more motivated, they become more autonomous. This allows you to trust them more – to use less of your time and energy telling them what to do and how to do it. Dr. Amabile's findings show that as long as the work is meaningful, managers do not have to spend time coming up with ways to motivate people. This frees up your time and attention to make a greater strategic contribution.

Your true north

Creating a deep and layered sense of shared purpose across your organisation is the linchpin for making your strategic execution performance a force that drives your business forward.

> With purpose, your strategic journey has direction – your enterprise has a strong sense of true north.

Your strategic activity doesn't require constant management attention to give it direction. It can serve as a beacon of light that inspires, guides and gives your strategy forward momentum. Your purpose can serve as a mirror in which to reflect on every strategic choice you make and future-focused activity that you undertake.

Shared purpose is one of the most important influences on your strategic performance – on your ability to translate strategy into operational reality and business results. Purpose sets the direction for your business's future-focused activities. It's the compass for setting the course of your strategic journey. It's the barometer for determining strategic importance – for setting the priorities for your strategic activity. It's the gauge for assessing whether your activities are making meaningful progress toward your strategic objectives.

For purpose to have power, it can't simply be held closely by a select few in the organisation. It can't be the solitary domain of the 'thinkers' in the business, who then tell the 'doers' how to apply their strategic thinking. This is when purpose becomes not simply a missing influence, but a detrimental one. This is when organisational change creates uncertainty and fear, which in turn breeds resistance. It is the birthplace of organisational inertia, which stands in the way of nimbleness and the ability to adapt.

To imbue purpose with power, it must be shared. Your people need to understand it and embrace it at a level that relates to their jobs: to how they go about their work every day.

A ladder up

When thinking about purpose and what represents value for an organisation, I am often reminded of the observations made in Steven Covey's book The 7 Habits of Highly Effective People*; specifically, around habit two: Start with the End in Mind.*

Value is all about starting with (and keeping!) the end in mind as project priorities are established, as decisions are made and as strategy is executed. This end is what he refers to as the 'first creation' – the future that we seek to step into. He makes the subtle point that as 'ends' go, it is no end at all but rather something we are always seeking to attain.

Covey uses the analogy of climbing a ladder to make the distinction between efficiency and effectiveness. Moving up the ladder quickly with a minimum of wasted energy is efficiency, but ensuring that the ladder is leaning against the right wall is effectiveness.

Much of what we value in business these days is the efficiency with which we do the work we have always done. Our strategic focus is on being better than the competition making what we make – on making it cheaper and faster with more features. This is what Covey refers to as the 'second creation': the work and activities that allow the first creation to be brought to life – to become operational reality.

Covey argues that the difference between the most highly effective people – and organisations – is that they don't make their first creation the default option: what they have done before. Rather, they start with an end in mind and then persistently and efficiently pursue the activity that will allow that end to be manifested.

Returning to our ladder, Covey makes the point that management focuses on efficiently climbing the ladder whereas leadership represents proper selection and positioning of the ladder. He goes on to quote the words of Peter Drucker and Warren Bennis to further this distinction: 'Management is doing things right; leadership is doing the right things.' He makes the point that leadership (the 'first creation') must precede management (the 'second creation') for any organisation to effectively meet its business aspirations.

So how does the ladder relate to the idea not just of purpose, but of shared purpose, in becoming a more adaptive, future-focused business?

First, begin by ensuring the ladder is leaning against the right wall. Only then turn your mind to climbing it as quickly and efficiently as possible.

Above all else, it is essential to ensure that everyone is using the same ladder.

Planning and prioritising

When your organisation has a shared purpose and a common understanding of what represents value for the business, you have the ability to differentiate that value. Then you can decide what is most important in the current circumstances and which strategic activities are the most critical in responding to those circumstances.

> Strategy becomes less about faithfully following a plan and more about making good decisions in prioritising your strategic investment of money, time and attention.

Your strategic planning can become an ongoing process of synthesising your current business environment and plotting the course for the next portion of your strategic journey – not just an annual activity that generates a 'plan.' You can use a clear purpose to re-assess your strategic priorities in light of the business change you're experiencing or can see coming over the horizon. Are your deliberate strategic activities still the right ones to focus on, or should they be adjusted slightly? Are there emerging issues or opportunities you should prioritise for better strategic positioning?

When this purpose is shared across your organisation, then all your employees are better positioned to recognise threats or opportunities as they emerge. This allows them to feed these observations back into your strategic priority assessments. Better still, they begin generate ideas on how to mitigate these threats or seize a particular opportunity to be translated into a project for strategic assessment.

Your entire organisation is thus better equipped to make decisions and course corrections on ongoing strategic activities without constant management attention. They can shape the activities, scope and deliverables as well as maximise the return of your strategic projects in a much more effective way when they understand the context of the outcome that the project is meant to deliver.

As your organisation's strategic maturity develops, your people will begin to shape their operational activities to deliver greater strategic value. They will understand the value of a positive customer experience in retaining and delighting existing customers. They will recognise the value of an innovative approach or a clever solution to a problem and will share these for strategic deployment across the business.

In this way, you start to close the loop – your strategic efforts not only improve the operational elements of your business, but your operational activities begin to shape your strategy.

Establish and experiment

One of the most important aspects of establishing a shared purpose is being clear that this adaptation will involve the entire organisation.

However, adaptation (or 'change') on a transformational scale can trigger the organisational immune system and release the dreaded 'resistance'.

Resistance is a fast-growing movement that rails against any sort of uncertainty because of all the certain harm it will do – people will lose their jobs, you'll break things that weren't broken, you'll chase your customers away to the competition.

One of the most effective antidotes to resistance is experimenting. Test a new idea or an alternative business approach in the relative safety of a laboratory (project!) environment. Use a proper scientific approach: establish a hypothesis around the intended beneficial outcome, then actively seek to disprove it. Use the people most affected by the change (and hence most likely to resist it) to conduct the experiment.

As with most experiments, there are three potential outcomes: you disprove your hypothesis, your hypothesis remains intact (i.e., NOT disproven) or you learn something completely new that makes the old hypothesis obsolete. Out of these outcomes, you'll gain one of two important insights: what is likely to work or what is likely to not work. Both are important clarifications when it comes to making decisions about strategic value.

With this clarity in hand, you can now determine what action to take next. This could include more experiments or moving to the operational stage.

The transparency of the decision-making process will deepen the collective sense of purpose with your people and break down the spread of resistance.

The next logical stage of a successful experiment is to operationalise your findings. Begin to test the approach or product in the hard-bitten world of operational reality. But don't make an all-or-nothing bet. Give your people an opportunity to work through the teething pains and improve it. Turn off the non-essential features or do a pilot test in one area of the business. Allow the inevitable missteps to present a challenge for your team to overcome rather than a failure for them to be ashamed of.

Testing should also be viewed through the lens of business value. Did it perform as anticipated? Was the value what you thought it would be? Were there unintended consequences that degraded value in other areas of the business?

If your testing can withstand this scrutiny, then it is time to think about scaling up to the operational level. By this time, you'll have reduced the level of uncertainty with the change. You'll have reduced the risk and disruption to the business. You'll have developed what John Kotter describes as a 'guiding coalition' of managers and users who should be advocating its value, all the while deepening its ties to your business purpose.

Translate, don't communicate

There is no doubt that shared purpose is an important element of culture. But it is just one element. This element also requires that sharing occurs in both directions if you are to shape a high-performance strategic culture. After all, having a thorough understanding of the business's purpose but no ability to shape or affect it is not a particularly strong cultural influence.

It is also extremely important that the business's leadership communicate the higher-level purpose: what represents commercial value and strategic intent. This can't simply be done through a single conference, meeting or 'note to staff'. It must be performed consistently and often through a range of communication pathways and messaging approaches.

This type of communication can't be boiled down into slogans that sit above the reception desk, dangle below email signatures or adorn posters in the breakroom.

They need to be authentic and delivered in terms that your people (and your customers!) can understand and relate to.

They also must be embodied in the way that your leadership goes about their business. We communicate not just with our words and the media content we produce, but also with our actions. Your people will value what they see their leaders value, not what they're told they value. So, an important aspect of creating shared purpose is ensuring your leaders are truly aligned with the collective view of business value and will subordinate their personal agenda to the creation of strategic value. Similarly, as a business leader you need to be aware of how you prioritise your strategic work. If you routinely elevate the importance of the immediate – the short-term results – over that of future-focused activities, then you are clearly communicating where value lies.

This means you must break down your high-level commercial and strategic objectives into areas of improvement and opportunity. These areas then need to be shaped into specific initiatives – projects – that have scope and outcomes.

This allows your organisation to translate the conceptual ideas of purpose and value into the concrete world of actions and activities that no amount of communication could ever accomplish. By constantly refreshing and maintaining this relationship between projects, improvement opportunities and business value, you maintain your people's connection with your overall strategic intent. But you also establish this glacier-like nature in your strategic approach. Your projects are constantly moving – appearing and falling away. Your improvement opportunities are shifting and adapting more slowly, but are always moving in the same direction. The overall business purpose is much more established, but by no means stagnant – its dynamism is much subtler but always there.

Translation is a more important mechanism for creating shared purpose. This means translating strategic intent into meaningful work your people can engage in.

Rhyme and reason

In 2014, I was asked to help shape the delivery environment on a $250 million oil and gas construction project. The construction company was close to completion on a nearly identical project that was substantially over-budget and a year late. Their regional manager wanted to ensure they were more intentional about influencing performance to avoid repeating the results of the earlier project.

So we set about operationalising their teams more effectively and putting in place an execution framework that treated interim milestones like strategic objectives and the workflows leading to these objectives as mini projects.

But there was one significant problem – there was no rhyme or reason to the way that the workflows and their associated interim milestones related to one another.

So, like many construction teams, the work fronts they chose to work on were those that were most available – the easiest to start and to demonstrate substantial progress on. Rather than determining then focusing on the highest priority work, they focused on starting as much work as possible. After all, a work front opened up is 'value earned' – to quote a much-used project management metric.

The fallacy in this approach is that the value of project work cannot be measured in construction dollars. Its value changes based on its strategic priority: the performance constraints that it removes or the future work that it enables.

So we set about trying to co-create a delivery strategy for the project that would allow the team to understand the strategic priorities – how they wanted to move through the site, how they wanted to layer the trades and the order they wanted to start up the various plant process units and systems.

The Project Director was a particularly recalcitrant Irishman who was firmly entrenched in the 'command and control' management ethos. He considered this strategic development exercise a monumental waste of time, insisting that 'the fecking strategy was in the program and budget – they just needed to fecking follow it.'

He showed impressive commitment to this belief in the way he assessed the progress of his team. 'Why aren't yer working on these fecking foundations?!' When informed that delivery of the equipment that sat on the foundations was much later than the equipment foundations they were working on and, hence, these had greater urgency, he was emphatic: 'I don't care! The program says you're meant to be working on this, so I want a crew working on this! Work on both of them!'

In the robust discussions we had on the subject, I explained that you couldn't extract a strategy from a budget and schedule.

When your people don't understand your strategy, then you have no strategy.

Absent an understanding of strategic value, there's no way to prioritise activities and no basis for making improvement decisions. Inevitably all you're doing is keeping busy – maintaining the perception of progress rather than making meaningful progress.

Then co-create

This process of translating strategic intent into concrete activities is all the more powerful when it is a process of co-creation. By involving your people in both shaping the improvement opportunities and identifying the projects to help realise those opportunities, you get two important benefits:

1. It generates ownership that helps to create a shared purpose.
2. It allows you to leverage the knowledge and experience of your enterprise to create better strategic activities.

When managers define the strategic work that needs to be done but remove the need to shape that work or make decisions about it, people quickly lose motivation to create or make decisions, which severely inhibits progress. When the people who will perform the strategic work have a hand in shaping it, they are much more invested in its success. They will be much more likely to see it through.

Your middle managers and senior staff have the best working knowledge of where improvements will have the greatest business impact. They're an untapped font of knowledge about where potential business opportunities might be lurking – they often just see them as opportunities that would be too hard to realise.

Your front-line staff are an important source of ideas about how your areas of improvement and opportunity might be translated to the operational environment. These ideas can be shaped into projects that clear the path for improvements or opportunities to follow. As your front-line staff will likely be implementing the resulting operational changes, it is important that their needs are addressed if the maximum efficiency, product or customer benefit is to be achieved.

There are certainly risks that what they see as possible may be limited by their history – what has always been done. But if you grant them the freedom to expand that possibility, they will surprise you with their insight.

This allows your purpose to be shared in both directions. It allows leadership to flow across your organisation – from top to bottom and bottom to top. Or, as I prefer, from the inside out and from the outside in.

Purpose isn't a secret that you let your people in on – it's a tribe that everyone is a member of.

Projectify points

1. Purpose is what connects your business and its people to what is strategically and commercially important – your WHY.

2. With it, your strategic journey has direction – your enterprise has a strong sense of true north.

3. To imbue purpose with power, it must be shared. Your people need to understand it and embrace it at a level that relates to their jobs – to how they go about their work every day.

4. This type of communication can't be boiled down into slogans that sit above the reception desk, dangle below email signatures or adorn posters in the breakroom.

5. As important as communication is, translation is a more important mechanism for creating shared purpose. This means translating your strategic intent into the actions and behaviours of your leaders, and meaningful work that your people can engage in.

6. More important is that by leveraging your entire organisation when framing your strategic activities, you get a deeper, more diverse perspective on the best way to manifest your purpose.

Conclusion

As you've just seen, projectifying your business's strategy allows you to continuously move the business forward in tight, iterative loops of test or prepare, implement and scale.

This creates a strategic environment that has momentum – where action drives clarity and direction. It means your strategic activities more consistently yield outcomes, which help to inform the strategic activities that follow. It also allows your strategic progress to be squarely focused on those projects of the greatest importance to the business.

By putting your people at the heart of the strategic development process you improve the quality of the transition from strategic intent to operational reality. You minimise the risks to your existing business and increase the customer-centric focus by taking advantage of your people's superior understanding of the operational environment. You also reduce the uncertainty associated with organisational change that can generate people's resistance – both by making them a part of the change and by making change in a progressive, controlled manner.

To be nimble enough to successfully evolve with the pace and pervasiveness of change in today's business environment, you can't afford to be incremental (or, worse yet, sequential) about engaging your employees, improving the business, and building new capabilities.

You need to do all three at the same time. Projectifying your strategic improvement creates layers of developmental activity, each building upon the others to continuously shape your business for the future you hope to create.

- The project framework provides the engine for a strategic cycle of planning/execution/thinking/re-planning that ensures you are constantly improving and adapting for the business future you want to create. It also creates a strategic feedback loop that generates ideas and insights that help shape your company's overall strategic agenda.
- This routine builds strategic capability – your project muscle – so you get better at doing projects and start doing better projects. As your project skills improve, your people experience meaningful strategic progress that creates an upward spiral of creativity, productivity and collaboration which, in turn, establishes fertile ground for innovation and adaptation in meeting business challenges and capturing emerging opportunities.
- By actively engaging and empowering your people to help shape the future of the business, you increase the strategic bandwidth of the organisation as a whole. The inside-out (rather than top-down) leadership necessary to successfully projectify your strategic endeavours increases your leadership bandwidth as more of your people are asked to lead. The improvements driven by your strategic activities create greater capacity bandwidth for taking on future-focused projects. The intrinsic motivation created by this empowerment shapes a strategic culture that thrives in both buoyant markets and challenging ones.

To take advantage of the synergies between these developmental layers, you need to be deliberate about maximising the three influences on strategic performance that we have discussed:

1. Empower your team.
2. Follow your project framework.
3. Share your purpose.

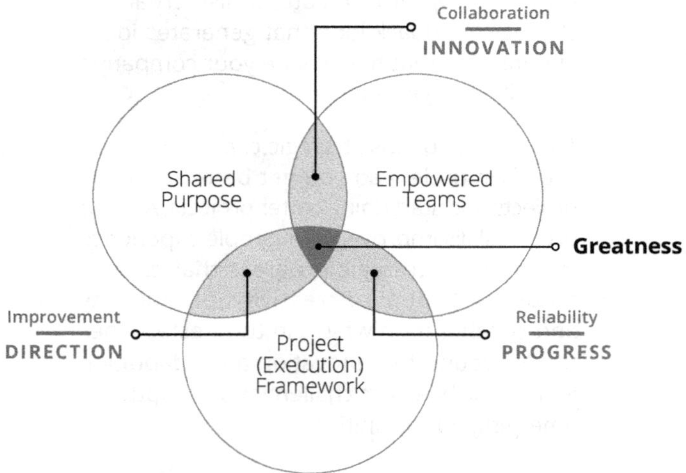

Importantly, these three influences are always impacting your ability to make meaningful strategic progress. You don't get to choose whether they're influencing your strategic impact – they're always an influence that can be either positive or negative. They determine whether your organisation is reactive or adaptive. The choice you make as a leader is to understand and maximise the positive aspects of these influences.

The real magic lives in how these three influences interact with each other.

When an empowered team is given a project framework that helps them undertake their project work effectively, you get reliability – you're able to consistently and progressively make meaningful strategic progress: day-in, day-out. You allow your people to get good at doing their strategic work. You give the people doing that work an opportunity to take control of their workplace and steer it toward what the organisation values.

When a properly configured project framework serves a shared purpose, you drive strategic improvement. When you compare the value that you want to deliver – the outcomes, the strategic objectives and the human interactions – against what is actually happening in the strategic execution environment, you find the basis for improvement: what improvement needs to happen, how to affect that improvement and the relative value of your improvement activities. Conversely, by applying a well-understood purpose to your strategic projects, you create strategic direction – you ensure that your strategic activities are focused on the most important improvements.

Collaboration lives in the interaction between shared purpose and an empowered team. True greatness is driven by effective collaboration. That's where management and the workforce combine their individual strengths and capabilities in a powerful way. It's where business and its people come together to create amazing things. It's where you create workplaces that people want to come to every day. It's where innovation lives, because innovation is the highest form of collaboration. Someone has a good idea... the organisation is astute enough to listen and see that it has value... the team is empowered to turn that idea into operational reality.

I like to think of each of these influences as balloons. You can choose to leave each of them flaccid with the traditional strategic approach of planning and analysis – having minimal overlap and, as a result, minimum strategic impact. Or you can fill them with energy and maximise their sphere of influence. This takes full advantage of the interplay between these three key influences and maximises the strategic progress constantly being brought to bear on your business.

When you can bring together empowerment, a meaningful operational framework and purpose in a unified way, that's where you create greatness – a great business that thrives in any environment and the great workplace that underpins any great business.

That's where you create a thriving, sustainable enterprise that doesn't just adapt to any business environment, but prospers.

What is certain is that the ideas in the book are not 'magic fifi dust' – you can't simply sprinkle them across your organisation and suddenly become the nimble, adaptive enterprise that you aspire to. It takes effort and it requires leadership energy and attention. It will be harder than continuing to do what you have always done because you'll be asking people to think, act and perform in new ways.

New is always harder than the status quo – at first. New will always seem to be less useful and to deliver less value than the status quo – at first. Learning and applying new things will be clunky and you'll likely stumble and fail – at first. As a leader, you will likely second-guess your organisation's ability to successfully apply these techniques – at first.

But progress will come – you'll start to see meaningful strategic activity. The three layers of development will start to make a shift in the adaptability of your business – resistance will melt away and a calmness will set in around change. Your leadership focus will move from constantly managing crisis – downside risk – to sifting through opportunities to identify the most valuable.

A client of mine, the field services division of an electric utility, were at the strategic exploration stage of developing their strategic roadmap. We were conducting a session to engage their field leaders in identifying the projects that would allow them to realise their strategic improvement opportunities.

The field services management team started to become concerned with the level of strategic engagement that we were asking of their teams. They were too operational for this sort of high-level thinking. They were too occupied with the day-to-day to look forward into the future. They were too cynical to believe that their ideas would be valued by management. The management team was worried that this workshop would fail to engage them and end up a huge waste of time.

My advice to them was simple – trust your people. Trust them and they'll repay that trust.

They did and the field leaders delivered 47 high-quality project ideas across 10 improvement opportunities. In the following six months, they successfully completed 12 of those projects – all the ones that they undertook – and not only delivered significant value against the business's strategic objectives, but started to slowly engage other areas of the business in the projectification movement.

So if you want to get started projectifying your strategy, start with trust – start by trusting your people. If you trust your people, they will repay that trust with valuable strategic insights into the inner-workings of your business.

Trust your people and they will repay that trust with their attention and commitment to the future you want to create for the business. Trust your people and they will repay that trust with their trust – they'll follow you where you want to lead.

Trust your people
and they will repay
that trust by creating
something 'amazing'.

Sources

Chapter 1 – The case for change

Shih, Willy. (Summer 2016). *The Real Lessons from Kodak's Decline.* MIT Sloan Management Review.

Rogers, Everett M. (1962). *Diffusion of Innovation Theory,* Simon & Schuster.

Moore, Geoffrey A. (1991), *Crossing the Chasm: Marketing and Selling High Tech Products to Mainstream Customers*, Harper Business Essentials.

Gladwell, Malcolm. (2000). *The Tipping Point: How Little Things Can Make a Big Difference Little*, Brown and Company.

Chapter 2 – An illusion of certainty

Ohmae, Kenichi. (1982). *The Mind of the Strategist: The Art of Japanese Business.*

Mintzberg, Henry. (1994). *The Rise and Fall of Strategic Planning.* The Free Press.

Kaplan, Robert S; Norton, D. P. (2001). *The Strategy-Focused Organization: How Balanced Scorecard Companies Thrive in the New Business Environment.* Boston, MA.: Harvard Business School Press.

Dye, Renée; Sibony, Olivier. *McKinsey on Finance Quarterly* (Autumn 2007), Issue 25.

Chapter 3 – A two-way bridge

Mills, Quinn D. (Summer 1996). *The Decline and Rise of IBM.* MIT Sloan Management Review.

Gerstner, Louis V. (2003). *Who Says Elephants Can't Dance? Leading a Great Enterprise Through Dramatic Change.* Harper Business.

Gallup, Inc. (2013). *State of the American Workplace: Employee Engagement Insights for U.S. Business Leaders*, Survey Results.

Aon Hewitt. (2014). *2014 Trends in Global Employee Engagement,* Survey Results.

Chapter 4 – Empower your team

Fussell, Chris; Silverman, David; McChrystal, Stanley A; Collins, Tantum. (2015) *Team of Teams: New Rules of Engagement for a Complex World*. Penguin Publishing.

Taylor, Frederick Winslow. (1911). *The Principles of Scientific Management.*

Henderson, Michael. (2009). 'Corporate Anthropology'. TedxAuckland.

Cook, Peter. (2013). *The New Rules of Management*. John Wiley.

Pink, Daniel. (2009). *Drive: The Surprising Truth About What Motivates Us.* Canongate.

Amabile, Teresa, and Kramer, Steven. (2011). *The Progress Principle: Using Small Wins to Ignite Joy, Engagement, and Creativity at Work,* Harvard Business Review Press.

Edmondson, Amy C. (2002). 'Managing the risk of learning: Psychological safety in work teams'. Harvard Business School.

Duhigg, Charles. (2016). *Smarter Faster Better: The Secrets of Productivity in Life and Business.*

Chapter 6 – Share your purpose

Sinek, Simon. (2009). 'Start with Why'. TEDx talk.

Amabile, Teresa, and Kramer, Steven. (2011). *The Progress Principle: Using Small Wins to Ignite Joy, Engagement, and Creativity at Work,* Harvard Business Review Press.

Covey, Stephen. (1989). *The 7 Habits of Highly Effective People.* Free Press.

Kotter, John. (1996). *Leading Change*, Harvard Business Review Press.

The end...
but the journey
is just beginning...

Thank you for investing your valuable time and attention into this book.

I hope it tweaked your thinking and begins to open new perspectives on the nature of strategy and the role your people should play in making it come to life. Mostly, I hope that you see this as not the end but as a beginning – the beginning of a movement to create something exceptional in your own business.

The nature of strategy-making, as I've laid it out in the preceding pages, is that any given moment is merely a waypoint in an ongoing journey. A journey that is continuously reassessed and refined to evolve your business into a better version of the one you have today.

Books only capture a point in time in the evolution of an author's thinking – their creation. So by the time you finish reading this, it is likely that my thinking and experiences mean that I have moved on to bigger, bolder ideas. Your thinking and experiences in applying some of these ideas might provide insights that evolve the collective consciousness of everyone that believes in the power of projectifying strategy to drive their business forward.

I'd love to stay connected with you – to share my evolving ideas and curate your experiences as we re-think the future of work and the workplace – together.

My email newsletter and blog are great ways to stay in touch with the latest thinking in turning strategy into action and harnessing your people's strategic leadership. You can sign-up for free at jeffschwisow.com/subscribe.

Also, please send me an email if you have some specific experiences or insights that you want to share. I would love to hear from anyone has taken these concepts into the strategic wilderness.

Finally, I speak and consult globally on all things projectifying, so let me know if you're looking for a guide, cartographer or Sherpa to support you on your strategic journey.

Over to you now – go start using projects to become the business that you aspire to be.

Go start creating greatness!

Jeff

Contact me:

jeffschwisow.com
info@jeffschwisow.com
au.linkedin.com/in/jeffschwisow
@jeff_schwisow

www.ingramcontent.com/pod-product-compliance
Lightning Source LLC
Chambersburg PA
CBHW070715220326
41598CB00024BA/3164